# THE THINGS WE

**BLAKE**

Published by Blake Publishing Ltd,
98-100 Great North Road, London N2 0NL, England

First published in Great Britain in 1993

ISBN 1 85782 015 0

British Library Cataloguing-in-Publication Data: A catalogue
record for this book is available from the British Library.

Typeset by BMD Graphics, Hemel Hempstead

Printed by Cox & Wyman, Reading, Berkshire

1 3 5 7 9 10 8 6 4 2

## ACKNOWLEDGEMENTS

Putting this book together has been hard work, lots of fun but undoubtedly it owes much to the input of other people. John and I are truly indebted to all of them for their time, help and support. So, without whom...

To each and every one of the contributors to this book, writers, cartoonists and celebrities who understood the message, wholeheartedly supported ROC, and gave so willingly, generously and brilliantly of their time, a long, heartfelt thank you from both of us.

A special thank you to John Blake for his enthusiasm and terrific support all along the way and for the same reason cheers and thanks in abundance to Cathy, Rosie Ries, Nick Smurthwaite, Gray Jolliffe, Siobahn Allders and Penney Folkerd-Hobbs.

Love and thanks to all of you, and especially to *you* for buying this book.

Frankie McGowan, 1993

Last year, Angela, my wife, died. We had been married for twenty two years and we had two lovely teenage daughters, Joanna and Laura. In early springtime, Angela had gone into hospital to have a routine operation during which her doctors discovered that she had extensive ovarian cancer. Angela's life ended sixteen brief, terrible weeks later. She was just 45.

There had been no symptoms to alert us to her illness. She appeared to be perfectly healthy, enjoyed her life so much, was full of fun and laughter, and was deeply loved.

Throughout all our years together, the good times, the bad times, the smiles and tears, the Easters and Christmases of life, she had always been so close to me and our extended family. To listen, to help, to console, to counsel, to laugh, to love. And now she was there no longer. She had slipped away to be with God. And we all miss her so very much.

Angela loved to help others and so, after she had left us, we knew that it would be her wish that we should do whatever we could to try and help prevent other wives, mothers, daughters, sisters, from losing their lives to this terrible disease. It claims over four thousand women in Britain each year. That's ten every day.

And so, my sister, Frankie, and I, together with our family and friends, including John Cullen (known as JC), established ROC (Research into Ovarian Cancer). JC lost his mother, Pamela, to the disease, also last year.

ROC is a national registered charity which supports a

research unit based at The Royal London Hospital led by Consultant Surgeon David Oram, and Dr Ian Jacobs. The unit is trying to develop a simple blood test which together with ultrasound will detect the disease five years before symptoms appear and while it is treatable in almost every case.

We have established ROC for the deep love of Angela's memory.

This book came to be compiled because we knew that many other people would have stories to tell of things that they have done for love and so we asked if they would tell you about them. This they have done and their unique and considerable talents have combined to produce a collection of wonderful memories, some poignant, some sad, some hilarious. Their recollections cover the whole gamut of human emotions that touch each of us through love.

Frankie and I are very grateful to everyone who has been involved and who have donated their time and contribution freely. All profits from the sale of this book will go directly to ROC.

If you would like to make a donation to ROC or to help in any way, contact us at The Royal London Hospital, Whitechapel, London, E1 1BB. Tel: 081-789 1406.

Thank-you very much.
John McGowan Co-Chairman of ROC 1993

Her Royal Highness The Duchess of York whose books include
*Victoria and Albert: Life at Osborne House; Travels with Queen
Victoria* and *Budgie The Helicopter Series.*

•

The love I give to my children and the love they show
in return is something quite unique which brings
harmony and growth to my soul. I still cannot quite
believe the magical blessing of children. How is it that
only nine months of pregnancy can produce such a
miracle that develops some of the greatest friends you
could ever have?

My children tell me the truth about myself, yet their
love is unconditional. At times you do not like their
frankness – especially when you have spent a long time
getting ready for an occasion only to be told that you
would look much better in Tinkerbell's wings or Peter
Pan's pixie boots.

They hug me when I feel blue and make me smile when
life seems in despair. There is a freshness and sincerity in
their faces which always reassures me. So, for me, what I
do for love is to nurture my two beautiful children
because in return they enrich and lighten my life.

**Richard Branson, entrepreneur, owns one hundred companies
in fifteen countries including Virgin Atlantic Airways as
well as being trustee of several charities.**

•

I met this lovely lady who worked as an assistant in a
bric-a-brac store. The only way her boss would allow
me to come and see her was if I bought something every
time I visited.

The courting and visits went on for 90 days and my
houseboat finally sank from the weight of the many items
of bric-a-brac I had bought from the store.

Still she felt rather responsible and once it was dried out
agreed to move in with me. Two rather lovely children
followed – worth every bit of bric-a-brac.

Tim Satchell, Fleet Street diary editor and freelance
journalist, has written biographies of the Duchess of York
and Fred Astaire.

•

Have I told you how and why I walked through five
miles of snowdrifts to not much effect?

Timing is all. If you're trying to make babies, your
helpful doctor will even give you some none-too-pleasant
pills 'to stabilise things'.

It was a pleasant winter's afternoon when I left
London. A song on the radio, a couple of bottles of
champagne in the boot. She had gone ahead to her
mother's home in the wilds of mid Devon.

The flurries of snow started slowly, the traffic gradually
thinned. By the time I reached the Exeter turn-off on the
M5 my car was alone in a sea of white, but there was
sudden perspective created by road signs, so I pressed on.
Five miles later only guess-work told me where the road
was – I aimed between the trees. Hoped.

Nose to windscreen, peering through whiteness on the
edge of Dartmoor. Finally the car limped and skidded,
how I don't know, into a straggled village where I crawled, frozen, frustrated in to a roadside pub.

The pub didn't shut that night. You couldn't get out of
the front door, the drifts were so deep.

Next day, ignoring all advice, a lorry and – a few
hundred yards behind – myself crawled on. On the A30

outside Okehampton I reached the farm of a former diplomat and abandoned my car. It was New Year's Eve. No one was going anywhere, so we drank a bottle of champagne and were in bed by ten. In the morning Paul said he'd get my car started with his tractor.

The tractor wouldn't start, the diesel fuel was frozen to a jelly. So I set off on foot. I had a church, some roads and a couple of large houses as guides. Paul reckoned it was about five miles as the crow flies.

You couldn't see most hedges under the snow blanket, progress was slow, falling deep into the unknown was frequent, clothes and boots were quickly sodden. Had abandoned all, but still had the second bottle of champagne bottle in a Harrods, carrier bag, which tore on branches. I didn't see or hear anyone, not even any birds.

I later learned that I hadn't been unnoticed. Farmers had come across half-covered footprints and phoned ahead that I was on my way.

The grey skies were growing dark. I was concerned lest I didn't find some sign of life soon. I thought that hypothermia might not be too bad an option, knew that coldness numbed the tiredness till the body slowed to a stop. But then unexpectedly I could see the twinkling lights of windows. Inside the house, the welcome, as well as the food was warm and comforting.

There was still one day to go on our calendar. Come, she said, let's go to bed.

It really is possible to go to sleep when one's head touches the pillow. And when the female is awake and aware and the male is frostbitten and comatose it's also pretty exasperating.

We missed that month. And it was a while before there was a happy ending. But there was.

Jeffrey Archer (Lord Archer of Weston-super-Mare) politician, playwright (including *Beyond Reasonable Doubt*) and novelist, the latest of which is *Honour Among Thieves*.

•

I think the most frightening childhood memory of my life was a journey from Weston-super-Mare in Somerset to Leeds in Yorkshire. The purpose of the journey was to spend Christmas with an aunt and uncle who were school teachers in North Allerton and as I had never travelled beyond Bristol or Bridgewater I looked forward to the day with much anticipation and relish. My grandmother was one of those early drivers who had not acquired a licence and had she ever taken the test she would have undoubtedly frightened the examiner out of his wits.

We left Weston-super-Mare in the morning in a large green Morris Oxford. My grandmother drove, my grandfather and mother in the back while I had the honour of sitting in the front, decades before anyone had thought of seatbelts. My grandmother, like myself, rarely travelled beyond the environs of Weston-super-Mare and for her the roundabout was a new fangled invention which she had not encountered before. We discovered the first one some seven miles outside my home town over which she happily drove straight across the middle and carried on in a northerly direction. We encountered twenty three such

15

obstacles set unnecessarily in our progress on our route between Weston-super-Mare and Leeds, and my grandmother crossed all of them in a manner which would have pleased Hannibal.

On arrival in Leeds, my grandfather who had learnt several years before not to speak, my mother who was not listened to when she did, and I who did not murmur a word, breathed more than a sigh of relief when we eventually arrived at my uncle's front door in one piece. Once safely on the premises I ventured the innocent question of my grandmother: 'Surely one should go around roundabouts and not across them?' To which she replied with British certainty: 'Certainly not. What you must understand young man, is that they will never catch on,' a degree of logic with which I am quite unable to find fault.

We returned home by train.

Philip Schofield, Children's TV presenter and star of *Joseph and the Amazing Technicolour Dreamcoat* now touring the UK.

•

I took a girl to see The Comedy of Errors, which isn't the most romantic of Shakespeare's plays. So, after I'd seen her home, I sat up half the night trying to learn a romantic Shakespeare sonnet – 'Shall I compare thee to a summer's day?' – to impress her on our next date. I had a video of Peter Sellers reciting it on an old Parkinson chat show.

I saw the girl next day and I was just about to melt her heart with my poetic declaration when she told me she didn't want to see me again.

**Cliff Richard, singer, has sold 45 million singles and works for the Christian Development Agency, Tear Fund.**

•

That first morning in Bangladesh I must have washed my hands a dozen times. I was there on behalf of the Christian Development Agency, Tear Fund, and I made a beeline for every standpipe we passed, furiously washing my hands for fear of catching something.

Everyone in the camps we visited, even the babies, was covered in sores. I was trying to keep everyone at arm's length.

Then, as I bent down to one little mite, mainly for the photographer's benefit, someone accidentally trod on the child's fingers. He cried out and, as a reflex, I grabbed hold of him forgetting about the dirt and the sores. I remember now that warm little body clinging to me, and the crying stopped instantly.

A Third World image, previously sanitised and kept at bay by TV bulletins, became reality: a statistic became a person. Through what was to be an appeal for funds, I'd encountered an appeal for love. In that moment I understood how starved these children were of love as well as food. Parents hadn't the strength or the inclination to show it: survival was too exhausting.

I didn't know it at the time but someone had taken a picture of me, ashen-faced, with the little boy buried in my shoulder. Today an enlargement of that snap is one of my most treasured possessions. It hangs on the wall between my bedroom and bathroom where I cannot fail to see it and remember.

Alan Plater, award winning writer whose TV adaptations have included *Barchester Chronicles* and *Fortunes of War*. He is currently working on a screenplay for Sir Richard Attenborough.

•

Recently I read a review of my good friend, Alan Bleasdale's funny and ferocious play, 'On The Ledge' in which the critic said that Alan loved all his characters, especially the crazy ones: indeed, the crazier the people, the more Alan loves them. The message from the critic was that this was wrong in some way I don't begin to understand. Why bother writing plays about people you can't stand? Even the villains I write about have some redeeming feature; Obadiah Slope, in 'Barchester Chronicles' – memorably played by Alan Rickman – was bearable because he was funny and got his come-uppance in the end. Like Malvolio, he is sick with self-love and there is no known cure for that condition. Slope would have done well in the 1980's and ended up with a knighthood or a prison sentence – possibly both.

We do everything for love if we have any sense. It generally takes root in adolescence. There are in the world several middle-aged women who, when they were girls at our school, provoked me into writing poems about them. They never knew either about the passion or the poetry.

The poems were dreadful and I destroyed them all, swiftly and mercilessly. They made E.J. Thribb seem like

Shelley and were densely packed with lines like:

'Oh that we might walk life's highway hand in hand'.

Most of the lines began with 'Oh' – a very good reason for giving any poem directions to the nearest bonfire.

Love was never just about girls. I was a Northerner, born in Jarrow and brought up in Hull. I love both places still, though Tyneside remains the Country of my heart. Football has always been a central part of my family culture. On a rough estimate I must have watched Hull City play about a thousand times. On an even rougher estimate the breakdown of the results is:

Won 333, Lost 333, Drawn 333. Goals for: 999. Goals against: 999. The thousandth match was abandoned because of fog – a home game in the 1970/71 season. Viewed statistically, it has been a totally pointless exercise, which proves it must be true love.

It was in the adolescent period that another love affair started: with Jazz. This is another incurable passion. Curiously enough, it was caused by another aspect of love – filial. I loved my parents but needed something to rebel about – we had all seen the James Dean films and rebellion became compulsory. Jazz was a way of rebelling against my parents without upsetting them too much. They were more concerned when I grew long sideboards, hoping to look like Humphrey Lyttleton and/or Gerry Bowler, a fine and wacky Irish centre-half who played briefly for Hull City with a Celtic abandon that couldn't survive the austere Humberside climate.

Now I'm bald, after the style of Shakespeare but not too pushy with it, you understand, with grown-up children who have kids of their own, and *that's* a love to cherish: love of grandchildren. You draw elephants and play daft games until you get tired or they get sticky and then you hand them back to their parents: an ideal system.

All in all, it's a mighty catalogue, the things I've done for love: from standing in torrential rain watching a nil-nil draw between Hull City and Hartlepool United to standing on one foot hearing the Ronnie Scott Quintet play to an audience of 400 in an auditorium with an official capacity of 150: from gazing in wonder at great comedians like Jimmy James and Norman Evans and ending up actually working with Sandy Powell, to drawing elephants for any small child who comes within range; from standing in cold December winds with ten other people in the belief that this would produce Peace in Vietnam to sitting in The Gods at the Theatre Royal, Newcastle, to getting a stiff neck and a swift kick to the imagination watching Michael Hordern in Twelfth Night, the painful comedy that remains my favourite of the man's plays.

Shakespeare knew that you can't have laughter without pain and by the same token you can't have love without the pendulum swings into pain, despair and betrayal. If we write plays because we love our characters, it is also because we rage about what is done to them by society and its rulers.

But all that belongs to another, more solemn agenda. We are here to celebrate love, lousy poems and all. I didn't *mean* to write rotten poems; I simply wasn't clever enough to write good ones. In any case, even a bad poem, a duff football match, an unfunny joke or a mediocre jazz band does no harm to the human race, which is more than you can say about the people who run the show most of the time.

Let us remember the gospel according to the great Duke Ellington who used to say to the audience at the end of each performance: you are very beautiful, very gracious, very talented and we want you to know that we do love you madly.

**Richard Eyre, Director of the Royal National Theatre and director of many films including *The Ploughmans Lunch*. He is author of *Utopia and Other Places*.**

•

I sit in darkened theatres clutching plastic cups of tea until midnight or fatigue arrive, whichever comes first. I spend good summer daylight hours in windowless rehearsal rooms pacing the floor, talking at length about lust and litigation, judges and jail, vicars and virginity. I expose my work to critics, some of whom, with the sensitivity of a sledgehammer, point out where I have gone wrong. I've learned the Egyptian National Anthem, how to tap dance and the correct way to hold an Iguana, all in the name of love.

If love is a kind of madness, then I'm totally insane.

Niamh Cusack, classical actress who has played Juliet and Desdemona at the RSC. Her films include *Paris by Night* and she also co-stars in *Heartbeat* for Yorkshire TV.

•

L ike most people I know, I have done many ridiculous and humiliating things in the pursuit of love and the loved one.

When I was sixteen I had a serious crush on an intense young timpanist in my youth orchestra. D had frightened, gentle green eyes and a halo of fuzzy hair and I was his for the asking. After a few passionate discussions on life and music in coffee shops, culminating in nothing more than a chaste peck on the cheek, he invited me to a Charismetic prayer meeting. I wasn't sure what this would entail but it was definitely the 'date' that I had been angling for.

That fateful Sunday morning in my most feminine dress and clogs (do you remember when clogs were fashionable?), I turned up at the address my beau had given me. It was a large family house in a wealthy suburb of Dublin. I was greeted by two smiling, middle-aged women. E had a wordly look in her eyes and very clean teeth, while H seemed much more earth-bound and bossy. D was already having coffee (coffee *before* the service? Us Catholics never got coffee until after we'd done our praying) with some others from the group. He welcomed me with a gentle hand on my arm

27

(he *touched* me!) and introduced me to the others.

After coffee we were ushered into another room with chairs arranged in a circle. Someone read an excerpt from the Bible and then started to pray. Then another woman read a bit and she too started to pray. Others joined in. The disconcerting thing about these prayers was that they were in a strange gobbledy-gook of a language. Sometimes it sounded like Latin and then it would metamorphose into something different. At first I wanted to laugh but as all around me, including my beloved D, were deeply into the chanting with eyes firmly closed, I realised that they didn't see the joke. As the cacophony of muttering, singing and whispering grew I considered running away out of the room but realised that this would mean losing my heart's desire.

'Well,' I thought to myself, 'I'll join in too. I'll pray in Gaelic and nobody will know the difference!' So off I went muttering my repertoire of prayers with an ear to the general chorus so that I wouldn't be left on my own in my version. After an hour and a half of crescendo and diminuendo in the religious fervour, the meeting wound down to a peaceful and friendly silence. We then dispersed with fond farewells at the front door.

D left me to the bus. Not a word was spoken of the morning's events and with the usual peck on the cheek he made his escape. We never had another date.

It was only later that I learnt how Charismetics speak 'in tongues', the language of the holy spirit, a language of no earthly abode, and so only the genuine Charismetic can speak it. No doubt D knew what a humbug I had been and all romantic dreams were scuppered.

28

Jane Hardy, writer and journalist contributes to national newspapers and magazines including, *The Times, Guardian, Ms. London* and *Top Sante* and teaches creative writing.

•

I've done my bit for infatuation, certainly. The top left hand drawer in my old pine chest bears witness to that. As well as underwear, it holds a folded tissue containing – what? – a nearly invisible dark curly hair. Male. This dates back to two years ago when, in my mid-thirties and quite a time out of relationships, I developed a serious crush on my art teacher.

The difference between love and crushes is that with the former, you are prepared to give of yourself and generally with the latter, you want to own.

The opportunity to acquire a sort of relic of Liam came, funnily enough, during a life class. I'd just finished sketching the female form, he came and criticised what I had drawn, then as he stooped bending over the drawn breasts on my sheet of cartridge paper, he left a three-inch long hair on my jumper. I was so excited, I put it in my bag and enshrined it in Kleenex at home.

Similarly, I kept for a while a prescription signed by a doctor I was keen on. It was, incredibly, for KY jelly for my mother.

For love, I have behaved altruistically. I have typed poems and cvs for my current boyfriend. And I stayed for nearly three weeks in the Royal Masonic Hospital, West

London, in 1991 when my mother appeared to by dying.

This period was one of the most intense of my life. I entered hospital time. I ate in the canteen, talked to doctors and nurses, walked through the building – '30s liner design, becoming flaky – every morning to see a), if Joan had survived and, b), what I could do to make her eat something, anything. She had suffered side-effects from a heart drug, looked as if she had cancer and wouldn't eat or drink. I shall never forget making her a vegetable soup. Buying the carrots and onions and potatoes in King Street, getting permission to cook in the ward kitchen, running to and fro in unseasonal May heat and thinking if I didn't do it, she'd fade away. I made it, she didn't drink it, but she didn't die either. The happy ending, the tennis courts and players opposite, the illuminated cross in the hospital chapel, all spell to me an obsessive but true kind of love.

Mel Calman's cartoons appear in national newspapers and magazines. his books include, *It's Your Turn To Leave Me* and *How About A Little Quarrel Before Bed?*

Bruce Oldfield, international fashion designer started life
in a Barnardo's home is now one of the Princess of Wales
favourite couturiers.

•

About twenty-five years ago, whilst at teacher training college in Sheffield, I was due to go on a trip to the London Galleries with our art department. I was particularly keen to go because of a hot crush on a fellow student (unrequited to this day).

Unfortunately I missed the bus but decided that, by hook or by crook, I was going to London if only to sit next to her all the way back in the coach to Sheffield.

I started to hitch-hike down the M1 but luck wasn't with me that day and I finally arrived at the pickup point in Russell Square to see the coach pulling off the stand... I never told anyone about this little adventure, I felt, and still do, feel extremely stupid.

Phillip Hodson, journalist and counsellor is advice columnist for the *News of The World* and is author of *What Kids Really Want to Know About Sex*.

•

I was once completely besotted with a beautiful girl who had some intriguing, even peculiar ideas about how to conduct a relationship. For instance, she'd give me precise instructions about where we should meet, what time, etc, but I wasn't allowed to speak and had to follow her suggestions. In other words, she took the initiative. She got extremely turned on by this element of mystery and so did I – at first.

We lived in this fantasy world for some weeks. While it was very arousing, it obviously wasn't a very practical way to carry on. My boss didn't understand when I wouldn't talk to him in the office corridor because 'Tuesday was our day of silence'.

I also began to see (I was a bit young at the time) that her need for play-acting and mystery came from real difficulties in her personality. I wanted to develop the relationship but she was stuck in her fantasies. But I *loved* it while it lasted.

Yvonne Roberts, newspaper and television journalist, her
books include *Man Enough* and *Mad About Women*.
She is writing her first novel.

•

Each week, my cousin Cath, aged 18 and me, aged 10
years and nine months, were delegated to clean the
attic bedroom. Cath's older sisters, Peg and Jeannie were
responsible for the two bedrooms on the first floor while
my Aunty Min cleaned the ground floor. This included
the front room, kept for best, the sitting room, the size
of a caravan lounge, gleaming with brass and china
nick-knacks and 'the back' – the prefab kitchen with
corrugated iron roof which doubled up as the only bathroom and bolt hole for anyone who wanted to smoke an
illicit fag.

Muzak for the Sunday morning clean was provided by
the screams of the seagulls in this North Wales seaside
town – and the voices in the chapel next door.

*'Bread of heaven! Bread of heaven…'*

Plus Two Way Family Favourites turned up full blast.
The posh English voice of Jean Metcalfe would plaster
over all the lust and longing with banal messages from
outposts of the British Empire. 'Bill in Akrotiti sends all
his love to Nancy in Stockport and says it won't be long
now before he's home. The message is in the song.'

*'Each night I ask the stars up above, Why must I be a teenager
in love…?'*

'What's B.U.R.M.A.?' I'd ask Cath as we both lay on the bed while she wrote love letters to Bill, her fee-aan-saaay (the more syllables, the more significant the promotion from spinster to about-to-be-spouse).

'It's a place.'

'But Bill's in Yorkshire, not BURMA.' I persisted, a young pioneer in pedantry.

'BURMA is a place you go to when you're older.'

'How far is it from London?'

'Far enough for you not to know about it…'

Cath did a jive around the room with an imaginary partner. *Chantilly Lace and a pretty face… a wiggle in her walk… and a giggle in her talk…* Cath could wiggle, *really* wiggle.

She was born blonde but took to the bottle, bleaching with gusto from the age of sixteen. Now, she was almost cream haired. 'Is it natural?' a lad would occasionally ask.

'Natural?' Cath would say, 'Natural? Of course it's not bloody natural what do you think I am? A bloody albino?'

Cath always had an answer; a quip; a bit of backchat.

Cath and I were a team. 'Cleaning' the attic was a doddle. Switch on the hoover, spray a couple of squirts of furniture polish into the air – and lie on the bed for a good forty minutes or so doing nothing. Occasionally, Peg or Jeannie would catch us out. Once Cath concussed Peg on the bedhead because Peg said we were lazy cows.

Peg lay there pale-faced, skinny legged, her net petticoats stiffened with sugar standing to attention. She looked like an overturned standard lamp. 'Christ,' Cath said laughing, impervious to Peg's condition. 'I'd hate to be the bloody undertaker who lays you out.'

If it had been me who'd knocked Peg out, I would have been worried sick that I'd killed her. Not Cath.

In 1959, in a non-conformist, highly conformist society in which men didn't impregnate women, they miraculously found themselves 'in the family way' bringing shame and temporary excitement to the entire community. In 1959, a time when everybody cared what everybody else thought about what everybody else was doing, wearing, saying, Cath genuinely didn't give a damn.

'Now, she's a wild one, isn't she, dell?' They'd say to my Aunty Min. And, 'She's got too many brains for her own good, that girl.'

I affected to be totally, utterly unimpressed by Cath. She had breasts, I didn't. She had jokes, I didn't. Cath worked in an office – everybody else worked in the washing machine factory. Cath wore tight, short, white skirts, even in winter. She also wore the most up to date winkle-pickers; pale blue chunky knit M&S cardigans with whalebone buttons the size of saucers and when her hair was done, secured in place by a sticky iron cobweb of hair lacquer (one and sixpence from Woolies), and her pale apricot lipstick had been fixed and checked in the mirror over the fireplace in the lounge, she was A Star.

Every time some pea-brained adult asked me; 'And what do you want to be when you grow up?' I'd usually say, a creep to the last, 'A missionary doctor.' But honestly, what I wanted to be was Cath.

'Fancy coming out on Friday?' Cath asked casually during one of the weekend cleans.

'Out? You mean at night?'

'Yeah, I'll take you out for a treat.'

This conversation was difficult a) because I'd grown accustomed to the idea that 'nearly eleven' barred you from almost any activity that was remotely interesting, and b) I'd caught a glimpse of the inside flap of the most recent envelope dispatched from Bill to Cath. (I was always sent from the room while Cath hid her cache of letters). B.U.R.M.A. was written across the top and then a word was suspended from each letter like flypaper from a light bulb.

'*Be Undressed…*'

'Well, do you want to come out?'

'*Ready, My….*'

'We'll go to The Blue Lagoon in Llandudno. I'll buy you a milkshake and you can put some money in the jukebox.'

The Blue Lagoon had only been open a few months. It had one of the new cappuccino machines; it served two mouthfuls of coffee in perspex cups, it had stools on spindly legs and, above all, it had a jukebox. The *first* jukebox in Llandudno.

'*Angel…*'

'What will Aunty Min say?'

'She won't mind if you're with me. We'll just say we're going out to Bingo or something. It'll be smashing. Trust me.'

I always did because if Cath was there, there was also a good time.

'*Be Undressed Ready My Angel,*' The sentence suddenly made sense. Oh My God. I could feel myself go bright pink. B.U.R.M.A. Be Undressed Ready My Angel. It was a place you go to when you're older all right. It was *rude*.

Cath was packing up the letters, oblivious. 'I'll write and tell Bill that I'm out with you on Friday night. If it's you, he won't mind at all…' Bill and Jealousy, like egg and bacon, always went together.

'You take care of her, mind,' Aunty Min shouted from

the front door on the Friday as we ran like hell for the bus, laughing fit to bust.

The Blue Lagoon was a fug of smoke. Everybody knew Cath and acted as if I was invisible. I couldn't have been happier.

*'I had a girl, Donna was her name... Since she's been gone, I ain't never been the same...'* was being played over and over again, the juke box whirling and clicking to select the same 45, the whole performance neon-lit like fireworks on Coronation night.

Cath sat at the bar and ordered a cappuccino and a strawberry milk shake. Then, *she lit up a fag!* In *public*. Aunty Min would kill her. 'Want one?' she said, then laughed. 'Only kidding.'

Ten minutes later, Paul arrived. He was tall and slim and had a shock of blonde hair just like Cath's – except that I don't think his came out of a bottle. He might have been a real Albino but I couldn't see if his eyes were pink since he was wearing dark glasses. In February.

'Paul's got something to show me,' Cath said. 'I'll be back in five minutes. Gloria'll look after you, won't you dell?'

Gloria, behind the counter, with hoop-earings the size of lifebelts, looked at me suspiciously.

'You wanna something-a?' Gloria asked. I shook my head. I was the only nearly-eleven year old in the whole place. If I sat still long enough, I thought to myself, perhaps people would forget that I was nearly-eleven.

After half an hour Cath still hadn't come back. Perhaps this was a test. Cath was testing me out. I was happy. Happy to be invisible. Happy to be in on something – although what, I wasn't quite sure.

According to the clock in the shape of a Coke bottle top, Cath had been gone fifty-seven minutes when she suddenly popped up again, fizzing. 'Come on kid,' she said. 'Let's get some fish 'n chips.'

'Where's Paul?' I asked. Cath was struggling to get her engagement ring back on. Cath gave me a hug as we pushed our way to the door.

'Now, listen kid. Can you keep a secret?' I nodded. 'If anybody asks you, Auntie Min, Peg, Jeannie, Bill, if anybody asks you, say nothing about The Blue Lagoon. Say nothing about Paul. Don't say a word. Promise?'

'Who is he then?'

'Nobody, he's just a friend.'

'Why can't I say anything then?'

'Because if you do,' Cath said, 'I'll be bloody murdered.'

'Really?'

'Really.'

We came home on the last bus after a night to remember; cod and chips, a trip to the amusement arcade. I'd forgotten that Cath's life lay in my hands. I'd forgotten that if I really loved her – which I did – I'd have to lie. Not lie accidentally, spontaneously which I did all the time. But lie, *knowingly*. And who knows how God might react?

'And what time do you call this?' Auntie Min was waiting at the front door. On the table were cups of tea and ham sandwiches 'to tide us over' until the morning.

'So what have you been up to then?' Auntie Min asked as we sat around the fire. Cath gave me a wink.

'I've been to Burma,' I said. 'With Cath.'

© Yvonne Roberts 1993

Marjorie Proops, agony columnist at the *Daily Mirror* for over
forty years. Her autobiography, *Marje: The Guilt
And The Gingerbread* was published this year.

•

M y first great love tried, against the odds, to teach me
to play the piano. I was 15, confused about religion,
attracted to the Catholic Church when my music teacher,
an old man of about 35 with smouldering eyes and nimble
fingers, stirred my adolescent senses and I chose him
instead. I was heartbroken for two days when he departed.

Luckily Mr Pogerelski entered my life. He was about a
foot shorter than I but I looked up to him because unlike
most of the other loutish art students, he was very polite
and he saw me home after classes and carried my portfolio.
I never knew his first name and was once again heartbroken when I had to leave art school to try to earn a living.

Many years passed before I discovered real, grown-up
love after a few more false starts. The real thing hit me
when I'd been married for 20 years or so to a man I couldn't
love. And for a further 20 years, I participated in a secret,
illicit love affair with a colleague. It was a perfect relationship except that we couldn't marry and fulfil the dream
that lovers in this situation share.

Now that both he and the husband I betrayed are no
longer alive, I often wonder if such perfect, ideal love
could withstand the pressures and the aggro of everyday
life as distinct from life which is lived, it seems, on another

unreal planet. Would I have gone on loving this tetchy, fussy man if I'd neglected to wash his socks and Y-fronts? Would he have been so adoring if his dinner was late? Or charred? Would I have indulged his whims or he mine for ever and a day?

I will never know. And maybe it's just as well...

Gary Lineker, footballer, England Captain and former Spurs
star, is currently playing away in Japan.

•

Wherever I wander, wherever I roam,
  To Spain or Japan, where we now have our home,
I know it's peculiar, but number one task
When phoning to England is always to ask
For progress and news of the love of my life,
(apart from my family – my sons and my wife).
When summer is here and rain's not stopped play,
What is the score from the CRICKET that day?

Joss Ackland, theatre and film actor and star of numerous films
including *White Mischief*, *Lethal Weapon II* and
*The Hunt for Red October*.

•

Much as I disapprove of the Englishman's dispro-
portionate love of animals I suspect somewhere
deep down I too, have been affected by this lunacy.

When I was a young boy I was given some fishing tackle
as a birthday present. As I was an evacuee in Bedford
I took my new rod and line to the River Ouse where I
caught a fish, proudly took it home in a bucket, then
placed it in our bath where it swam back and forth.

My mother was furious when she saw it and told me to
get rid of it. So I returned it to the bucket, walked all the
way back to the river and threw it in. As far as I know it
still swims there today.

Over 50 years later my wife and I were staying in Italy
when we were plagued by rats and mice. Eventually we
put down some poison.

One morning I went to have a shower and there were
two baby mice obviously punch-drunk after tasting a
snack provided by Lucretia here. So I put them into a
cardboard box, drove out to the wheatfields and deposi-
ted them in the hope they would recover.

Maybe by now they have met up with the fish in
heaven, bragging about who had the narrowest escape.

Bryan Forbes, actor, director and writer. The contribution he has made to this book has been taken from his autobiography, *A Divided Life*.

•

The Blitz was over and we were allowed to return home during the holidays. My parents had found another house in Newbury Park near Ilford in Essex.

I can remember nothing of that first holiday, I can only recall the return to Cornwall. I caught the train back at Paddington, not labelled and dragooned as on the first occasion, not in fear of the falling bombs, but as somebody going back to familiarity after a break.

I occupied the same carriage as a ravishing young school girl, like me a returning evacuee, who wore the brown mortar board of a convent school and who proved to be just as vulnerable as myself. She was journeying to Newquay and destined to leave the train before me to catch another connection. Her name was Marguerite and I fell immediately and helplessly in love with her.

Love in one's youth is an endless purple passage and to attempt to disguise that fact is to deny the beauty and agony of a perfection that comes but once, for, to turn to Connolly, 'once only are we perfectly equipped for loving: we may appear to ourselves to be as much in love at other times – so does a day in early September, though it is six hours shorter, seem as hot as one in June.'

49

Was I 'perfectly equipped' for loving? I thought I was. The first and most urgent fear that possessed me, the fear that the homing journey would come to an end before I had managed to make the force of my emotion felt, was soon dispelled. We were told at Exeter that the train had to be diverted – there had been a bad crash on the main line between there and Plymouth, with the consequent delay of some hours.

I am compelled to warn those who are now expecting to read a variation of Frank Harris or *Walter's Secret Life* that, unlike those two sexual athletes, I did not fall upon the delectable Marguerite the moment the train pulled out of Exeter. I wish I had, for one of the keenest pangs of advancing middle age is the remembrance of chances lost. My thoughts were totally impure, my motives towards her unashamedly carnal, but I lacked that first requisite of the would-be seducer – opportunity. We did not have the carriage to ourselves. Being wartime it was crammed to overflowing.

I should perhaps anticipate my reader's curiosity and reveal that the attraction was mutual. Although I can understand my own feelings, since I want this to be an honest account of my life and tribulations, I cannot comprehend why the enchanting Marguerite gave me a second glance. Studying the Box Brownie snapshots of the period, I appear to have been something less than God's gift to convent girls. I had an absurd haircut and a perky little face devoid of character. I looked rather like one of the dust-jacket illustrations to Richmal Crompton's *Just William* series.

But apparently I helped to pass the journey for her, and oblivious to the other occupants of the carriage, we embarked on the first tentative voyage of exploration

which only erotic liars pretend to recall in detail. I have no
such details, alas; I cannot remember a single word we
exchanged, all I retain is the picture, blurred around the
edges, of a young girl trapped within that building grove
of Proust's imagination, who indulged me, made me
captive, enchanted and destroyed me and who now
still has the power to rekindle the ashes of a lost
personality.

She was, unlike any girl I had encountered before, soft
in outline, with that pampered loveliness that comes but
once. I began to make feverish plans, carrying on in-
coherent conversations which never began or ended,
while my mind evolved the most fantastic schemes. With
every passing minute I became more and more conscious
of the need to declare myself before it proved too late. But
at fourteen the words don't come. First love can only be
expressed in retrospect, and even then the middle-aged
poet distorts the past with experience. At the time it is a
race towards a winning post that never gets nearer, a
waking nightmare.

Somehow, I must have found the courage to ask for her
address. I have no doubt that she was more in command
of the situation than I was, for girls of that age are
infinitely more aware. Even then I must have had some
inner conviction that my pen would prove mightier than
my spoken word.

We eventually arrived at Exeter. She left the train
there and I journeyed on alone to Helston. I imagined
her arrival at Newquay, tried, like any other young
lover before me, to put myself in her place. I went over
every inch of my own battlefield, cross-examined and
reviled myself for the stupidity of my manoeuvres,
cursed my timid nature. I became convinced that all

was lost, that she would never think of me again.

The moment I was back in the vicarage I made the long journey an excuse to retire early. Secure in my own room, the door locked, I put pen to paper and wrote my first love letter. I recall that for her part she had given me a *poste restante* address, for her incoming mail was intercepted and censored by the nuns. I think I wrote to her care of a local newsagent.

The new term began the following day, but all was dross. I had posted my letter and for the next week I experienced those pangs so achingly familiar to anybody who has ever been in love. One makes allowances. The letter has to get there. Probably one just missed a post and therefore it didn't arrive the following day. So no need to panic. She would have got the letter on the second day... No, probably she couldn't get out of school to collect it. So allow another day. Now she has it, she has read it, probably two or three times, and is wondering how to reply in kind. My letter must have been a revelation to her, for what young girl could resist such extravagant expressions of adoration? Even if she *replied* that same night she couldn't post it that night. She would have to wait for a suitable opportunity. So don't expect anything yet. No news is good news.

But after six days, no news started to become the unthinkable.

Even so ... there could be other reasons. She could be ill. I wrote again in even more florid prose. I cribbed from Rupert Brooke, because all is fair. I made the excuses for her, I said that she wasn't to worry that I hadn't received a letter in return, because it made no difference to my feelings.

I waited again for a further week. My work suffered. I thought of nothing else. By the end of the second week I had convinced myself that she was dying, or worse still that my letters had been discovered and that her martyrdom at the hands of the nuns was in progress. My ideas of convent life were inexorably bound up in fragmented misconceptions gleaned from the turgid volumes of the lives of saints in Canon Gotto's library, I conjured up a startling vision of my beloved held captive, forced to deny me, doing penance.

Straightaway I began to make plans. I obtained a one-inch Ordnance Survey map of the district and planned the route I would take. Porthleven to Newquay proved to be some forty miles. Bright with my one desire, I obtained permission to absent myself on Saturday, carefully checked and oiled my bicycle, and retired early on the Friday evening.

I live as a jaded traveller now. A journey of seven thousand miles, is a jumbo-sized chore, a boring race against the clock. The daily fight along the M4 to London, even in the smoothest of limousines, adds another crease to my belly – a mere seventeen miles in an insulated box, and we grow old in the traffic jams, breathing nothing but our own polluted air. The soul is no traveller any more.

That day, that Saturday when I folded and packed my best suit into the holdall on my bike, my spikey hair watered into submission, setting out on such a journey of promise, my legs anxiously spinning the miles away... that feeling will never come again. Yes, of course the temptation is there – how satisfying to colour yesterday's sketch-book with purple splashes – and yet sitting here at my desk, burning more of my midnight oil, I can without remembered guile pinpoint every turn of the wheel, older but no wiser, setting out once again as a fool, and certain to return so.

I left Porthleven at first light and was through Redruth before ten, pushing the pedals relentlessly, sustained by anticipation of certain joys to come. By a quarter to twelve I stood on the high land overlooking the bay at Newquay. There I went behind a hedge to change my clothes. That accomplished, I cycled slowly into town.

The map fades. I retain nothing of the geography of the streets or houses. I remember that I enquired the location of the convent school. Presumably I dismounted near by. Did I eat lunch? I have no recollection. I know I waited, but how long I waited... Was the sun shining? Were there other people in the streets? Faded images. Negatives of snapshots that were never printed. But no suggestion of defeat, that much I do remember. It never occurred to me that I wouldn't glimpse her, that was inconceivable.

There was a sort of happy ending. She did appear, I did see her. At some point during that afternoon a group of school girls snaked out of the courtyard, marshalled by nuns, and Marguerite was amongst them. The projector flickers, the action is jerky, a few frames are missing, but I can discern from this distance in time the progress of that giggling column as it crossed the street to the cliff-top and walked down the steps to the beach. I followed at a distance.

From the top of the cliffs I saw the group arrange themselves on the sand, the nuns black against the virgin beach, sinister blobs in the midst of all the innocence. I had never taken my eyes off Marguerite, watching her as a sniper watches his selected victim.

The rest is banal. Pulp magazine fiction. I went in

search of some gift for her. I was blinded with love. I spent all my sweet coupons on a box of chocolates. I returned to the cliff. They were still there below me, but now I saw that Marguerite was sitting apart from the rest, almost as if she sensed my presence.

I walked slowly down to the beach, watching the guardian nuns carefully evey inch of the way. Taking a long detour once my shoes felt sand beneath them, I casually worked my way nearer to Marguerite. I dared not give any signal, I could only hope that she would look up and see me approaching.

I was almost alongside her before this happened. Then everything went very swiftly. All I could remember afterwards was that I no longer had the box of chocolates in my hand. I was filled with shame. It could only be that I had dropped it in the sand beside her, a panicky gesture, completely out of character with the suave lover of my preparations, but I could not bring myself to retrace my steps. Useless, drained, I walked on to the harbour and thence up another set of steps to the promenade. When I got back to the beach and looked down she was nowhere to be seen.

It was Tuesday before I received a letter from her. By then I had dispatched three, each one more passionate than the last.

Her letter was brief. She thanked me for the chocolates, which she said were scrumptious; she thanked me for taking the trouble to come all that long way, and she signed herself with love.

I was, of course, transported. Alone in my room I went from the writing-desk to the mirror over the basin, finishing a page of humbleness and then examining my face in reflection. It seemed scarcely possible that I had not changed. I started to wash with extra care. I felt the need to be perfect for her.

The following Saturday I received my second letter from her. It was a long letter and it returned my love in full. In it she outlined a plan for our next meeting. She was to receive a visit from an elderly cousin who, she assured me, would be sympathetic to our cause. Chaperoned by this adult, she would be allowed to go her own way for the entire day. It was to be perfection.

I was up at an unearthly hour that second Saturday. I completed my toilet with infinite care, arranged and rearranged my best shirt and trousers, saw that my shoes were polished then washed again.

We had arranged to meet a short distance out of the town and when I arrived on the high ground overlooking the long sweep of the bay, everywhere was calm and a warm and lazy breeze flew in from the sea to dry the morning grass.

She came punctually and her 'elderly' cousin – who proved to be a girl in her late twenties – wandered off after some desultory exchange of pleasantries, doubtless confident that her young charge was in no danger.

We were alone, and the summer day stretched limitless before us.

I have no faded snapshots of her, no mementoes, no trace whatsoever, and although my memory is as vivid as a badly stitched appendix scar, I have no recollections of the actual operation. All I can recall is that she was not wearing her school uniform when she greeted me and that she was the protagonist throughout the hot blur of that day.

We walked to a deserted beach and there, presumably, took some picnic lunch. I can't be sure. I don't remember going into any cafe. I found it difficult to look at her –

does that seem possible? We must have talked, we must have held long and involved conversations, so much is certain, and yet nothing remains. You would have thought that everything about that day would have stamped itself indelibly on my mind, but such is not the case. All that love I could so easily confide on paper vanished without a trace. All I can evoke again is that sickening feeling of inadequacy that burnt into me more fiercely than the sun, the rising panic I felt as the realization that I was allowing the precious minutes and hours to slip away without progressing my cause.

She was, I now realize, bored with me, irritated by my passive adoration. I suppose I was totally unprepared at such close proximity for the revelation her superb young body offered. She too had made her plans and she came wearing a flowered bathing costume under her thin summer dress. There, beside me on the beach, she stood and removed the dress, artlessly, casually, then sank again to the sand, turning inwards towards me so that the full lushness of her breasts brushed against my arm. Nothing in my far from timid imagination had conditioned me for the real thing. That revealed and sunburnt flesh so close to my seaward-turning head, that mass of tumbled hair falling to touch the first swell of unkissed breasts had too much reality and I was powerless. With infinite regret I record here that we never exchanged one fumbled kiss – she was chaperoned by my turgid purity that day and perhaps that is why I remember her more vividly than those in whose arms I later lay with fonder delights.

How did I take my farewells? Did I see the cousin again? Were any promises given? Was hope completely extinguished before the afternoon ended?

I don't know. I suspect I was even more stupid than these

recollections suggest. I began the long journey home, dissecting every incident with each push of the pedals. On one of the steep hills before Redruth I overtook an old woman bent with the weight of her shopping bag. I dismounted and went back to her and offered to carry her parcels. It was a deliberate action, not my good deed for the day. I was challenging God, I dared Him, in the face of my conduct, to shatter my happiness.

He gave me a completely Old Testament answer. A few agonizing days after that Saturday afternoon I got a brief note from Marguerite. In it she said that she did not wish to see me again, that she considered it a waste of time to continue our association, and she signed herself, With All Good Wishes, or some such cruelty.

There is a postscript. Two years after the events I have described I achieved a certain local fame by becoming the Question Master of the BBC's Junior Brains Trust. My photograph appeared in the now defunct *Illustrated* and I entertained certain conceits. Armed with these, I went in search of Marguerite. I remembered the town she lived in and went there. I enquired at the local post office and was given an address. It proved to be out of date, but the present tenants furnished me with the new one.

Boldness being my friend, I presented myself at her door. Her welcome, when she had recovered from her surprise, was quite genuine. My fame, such as it was, had apparently preceded me. We walked out together. I met her parents and she was taken back to Newbury Park to meet mine. For a few days we were inseparable, but as her enthusiams blossomed, so mine withered. Despite her beauty (for the early promise had been fulfilled) she no longer had the power to destroy me. I kissed her goodbye one evening and I never saw her again. Her letters to me went unanswered, so that all we shared in the end was a common cruelty.

Bernard Cookson, newspaper and magazine cartoonist has also illustrated *The Lighter Side of Today*, the *Great Disaster* series and is preparing *Willy the Whale*, a new comic strip.

•

I think by far the greatest influence on my life was undoubtedly Rupert Bear.

He was immensely likeable, clever, resourceful and was forever having exciting adventures. Mum and Dad Bear seemed ideal parents... loving, caring and just sufficiently indulgent to allow Rupert enough space to enjoy his escapades with his dear chums: Algy, Pug, Bill, Edward and Podgy. Life at the delightfully picturesque cottage in Nutwood seemed idyllic. The weather appeared to be always perfect... nobody was ever really disagreeable and I am convinced that Rupert's early influence on me was such that I suspect ever since I have been (albeit subconsciously), through love of him, trying to arrange my own life along similar lines to that of Rupert and his chums at Nutwood.

Jo Foley, writer, journalist and former editor of *Woman*, *Options* and the *Observer Magazine* is now a freelance writer.

•

We stood on the small hillside looking across the flat, fertile plain towards Macroom and beyond into the blue haze that was the county bounds between Cork and Kerry. This is where he wanted to be – buried with his father but looking towards Kerry where he had met my mother and where I had been born. 'Come on,' he said, 'It's going to rain and I want a drink.'

We moved off. I didn't want him to get cold or wet – he didn't have that long to live and when he did die I wanted it to be in bed, in the warmth, not on the rainswept path of a country graveyard. As I looked back at my grandfather's grave I could not help but smile. Daddy had done it again! Only he could have got me to his own grave with such natural ease plus such a fine sense of the theatrical.

Later as we sat in one of those old side-of-the-road Irish pubs which smell of turf fires and porter, I opened my second packet of cigarettes of the day. Neither he nor I felt any sense of irony in my behaviour. He was dying of lung cancer and I was smoking 60 a day. As I puffed away and sipped a glass of Guinness (I was driving), he knocked back the whisky and told stories as he always had, of times long ago, of people long since dead and of incidents that were somewhere between fact and fiction.

He was a wonderful story teller, always had been, and

with his soft lilting voice he could keep people captivated for hours. He also had a prodigious memory and could remember times, places, who said what to whom sixty years ago as if it had only taken place last week. He also knew hundreds of poems, stories and songs off by heart. One of my earliest and fondest memories is of clambering into bed with my Daddy on Saturday mornings where he would sing to me and tell me stories. Often he would make me cry because the songs and the stories were so sad. So poignant were his renditions that he would cry along. This would enrage my mother who thought it heinous to make a child cry! We loved it.

In between the weepies he taught me a lot of Wordsworth, a little Tennyson, a great deal of Yeats and some really suspect ballads. I must have been one of the few five year olds who was word perfect on Ode on Westminster Bridge and the Face on the Bar Room Floor.

So here the two of us were, having a last wander through the places of his life in Cork and Kerry. Even though we knew it was the last visit it was anything but a sentimental journey. For someone who practically invented sentimentality my father was not in the least mawkish about his own dying. And that rubbed off on me. I could think about it, talk about it and deal with it.

Nearly eight months later we were sitting together again talking and having a drink. This time I wasn't smoking, I had kicked the habit I had nurtured and loved for nearly a quarter of a century with five hours of aversion therapy. I had gone from three packs a day to zilch after the first session. I had, I thought rather foolishly, promised my father on the day we were told of his cancer that if he never smoked again I would give up at the end of the year. Nothing like shutting the stable door…

As I poured him another whisky, he looked at me with his slow sly smile 'I never thought you'd give them up,' he said. As I have explained there was nothing sentimental in the approach to his living, so I gave him back my slow, sly smile, 'I never thought I'd have to. I thought you'd be dead and wouldn't hold me to my promise.'

We clinked our glasses and there was very nearly a tear in his eye. He died later that year – at 1pm on Christmas Day. Such a fine sense of the theatrical! I have never smoked another cigarette.

Neil Kinnock MP contributes regularly to newspapers, TV and radio. His books include, *Making Our Way – Investing in Britain's Future* and his most recent *Thorns and Roses*.

•

She was blonde. She was sparkling. She was an angel. She captured my every thought. And, like me, she was mine.

For days I found excuses to arrive at school at the same time, to leave school at the same time. I grasped every opportunity to fool around outrageously, climb over spiked railings, walk along high, narrow walls. I would tell any story to intrigue her, fight any fight to impress her (I didn't get the chance), take any risk to enthral her.

Still she made no response.

Driven beyond all sane judgement I showed the ultimate boldness: I crossed the invisible line between the boys' junior school playground and the girls' junior school playground ... and held her hand.

It was a dare. It couldn't be resisted by anyone impelled by my passion and my mates goading.

Of course I was spotted. The riot of screeching laughter made that inevitable. In any case, what was the point of such reckless gallantry if it wasn't noticed?

This was the flogging fifties before the swinging sixties. Retribution came. A twelve inch ruler brought down with force, three – or was it four – times on my right hand. Did they know that it was the hand that once, for a fleeting moment clasped the divine fingers?

Perhaps not. It did not even seem to bewitch my beloved. I think she became attached to someone else. Anyway I gave up love for several weeks. And it was a long time before my heart took me across any invisible lines.

Keith Waterhouse, writer and playwright. He is the creator of *Jeffrey Bernard Is Unwell*, *Billy Liar* and *Waterhouse at Large* from which the extract in this book is taken.

•

A American book once published over here, *Teenage Romance or How To Die of Embarrassment*, reminds me how little the basics of young love not to mention young love-bites – change over the years.

Teenagers may dress differently, dance differently, tattoo their heads and talk a language resembling Iroquois Indian but they still worry about their hands sweating when snogging at the back row of the pictures.

They still light the wrong end of the cigarette and realise only after flashing on a winning smile that they have a piece of apple stuck between their two front teeth, and they still hang about in the chemist's then leave without buying anything.

Or so we are told by Delia Ephron who wrote this instrucive compendium, which contains two valuable pages on How To Hide A Pimple and another two on How To Worry ('Worry that you have B.O.... Worry that everyone hates you... Worry that in a long kiss you have to breathe through your nose and your nose will be stopped up...').

Some worries she doesn't mention. Nothing, not even the ordeal of Romeo and Juliet, can surely match the anguish of two shy young lovers wandering across a buttercup meadow in the shimmering sunset... both of them dying to spend a penny.

Then when – on the excuse of having a sudden craving for a bag of crisps – they do re-reach civilisation with its welcome public conveniences (what if they're closed?), they both go into the wrong one by mistake.

Worry is to the under-sixteens as bad feet are to the over-sixties. Girl virgins still worry about being pregnant and boy virgins about being impotent... and virgins of either sex still confide to the dressing-table mirror, 'I know you can't get it off lavatory seats but I think I'm going to make medical history.'

Lavatories, come to think of it, have always loomed large in teenage nightmares. It is more years ago than most of you have had hot flushes but I still remember the chest-gnawing embarrassment of coming out of the men's room in the Majestic Ballroom, Leeds, colliding with someone carrying a tray of lemonade and returning to my partner looking as if – well, as if I hadn't made it in time. There was nothing I could bring myself to say, there was nowhere she could bring herself to look, and we never saw one another again.

Beyond bathroom range, there are still traumas enough. There must still be the anxiety of waiting for a date outside the Odeon, knowing perfectly well that is was outside the Odeon where you said you'd meet and having a clear recollection of her/his last words being 'See you outside the Odeon – but she/he is now a full one and a half minutes late and are you absolutely sure you didn't say the ABC?

Can left-handed boys kissing right-handed girls ever be absolutely sure that they're not going to move their heads the wrong way and get involved in a nasty nose-collision like stags clashing antlers?

70

Don't teenage girls still wrestle with the eternal and insoluble dilemma that they'll be thought too easy if they do and too hard-to-get if they don't? And don't teenage boys still hope for a disturbance from a park ranger or peeping Tom before they're forced to go further than they know how to?

Then there is the enduring suspicion that she reads out the choicest bits of his love letters to her best friends... that he told all his mates what happened on the towpath that night and that's why they're all giving her funny looks... There is the fear that the boil on his nose might not have cleared up by six o'clock this evening... and that the wisps in her comb are a portent that all her hair is going to fall out... There is the ever-present possibility that though her parents are supposed to be in Majorca, the hotel burned down and they are going to walk through the door and switch the light on any minute... and that when she smiled at him after that tender moment, she wasn't smiling at all, she was laughing at him...

Hideous, perspiring, stomach-clutching days. And what wouldn't you give to live through them all again?

Penny Vincenzi, best selling author of *Old Sins*, *Wicked Pleasures* and the most recent, *An Outrageous Affair*. She writes a regular column for *Good Housekeeping* Magazine.

•

Romance, one might be forgiven for thinking, is, if not dead, then certainly a bit poorly. In an age when girls dance with girls and boys with boys, when the dinner bill is split between two credit cards and thanks for a nice evening pushed through a fax, one could well think that a relationship would proceed briskly from a handshake to a complete relationship without wasting time on anything soppy in between.

Reader, one would be wrong. Romance is alive and well and setting hearts a-flutter just like it always did. Indeed, I defy any heart out there not to flutter in sympathy with the stories I have to tell you.

Take my friend Francesca, for instance. Married to a film man, for more than a year or two, he rang her from Czechoslovakia (they make films in esoteric places these days) very early one morning to hear her sobbing. (You should understand she is not a great one for sobbing in the normal course of events.) She had flu, a temperature of 101; she had a crisis at work and simply had to get in; she had a child in hospital being de-tonsillised; life was truly tough. She put down the phone, struggled into work and was sitting at her desk at around midday, holding her throbbing head, trying not to sob some more, when her secretary came in and said, 'You've got a visitor.' It was her husband.

Now, before you dry your eyes over that one, try this: a young friend at university was hopelessly in love with someone, and went to a concert with him, and they heard Tchaikovsky's violin concerto together. Very emotional. Next day, still not knowing, she returned to her room, and found the record of the concerto placed tenderly under her pillow.

And then there was my friend Angela. A while ago, when living in maidenly bliss in Earl's Court, she found a rose tucked under the windscreen wiper of her car one morning. And the next morning and the next. Earlier and earlier she got up and finally she saw him: not a boyfriend, not a smooth city suit, but a workman digging up the road, who had fallen in love with her dizzy prettiness and continued to leave the roses until the road was finally filled in again.

And there was my friend Jackie, who even more of a while ago met a friend in a coffee bar (remember coffee bars?) once a week and, every time they went there, two young men sat and smiled at them and were obviously much taken by them, but being well brought up, apparently pursued the matter no further. And it came to pass that Jackie was invited to a party one night in the wilds of Stanmore or some such, and almost didn't go, but did; and when she got there, standing in the hall clearly waiting for her, was one of the young men. 'It worked', was all he said. 'What?' she asked.

'For the past six months,' he said, 'I have phoned up every single friend and described you to them, hoping that someone would know you. And I have been to every single party I've been invited to because I knew I'd find you at one of them. And I have.'

I liked the rather more simple story of my friend Sarah's boyfriend, who couldn't afford a taxi or even a bus after taking her to the cinema, but spent his last few pence on the evening paper, so she could put it on her head and keep dry from the rain.

My own romantic tale is of a boy (very handsome) I met at the school dance: we waltzed once or twice and then were parted as the clock struck 12. Thinking I'd never see him again, for we had not exchanged names, and knowing my heart was broken, I was handed a letter a few days later, addressed to 'The Tall Girl In Green With A Yellow Ribbon In Her Hair', which says a lot for my sartorial skills, but never mind. We met and I thought he was awful, but it didn't spoil the romance of the gesture.

Some of the best gestures are quirky, not predictable at all: Daughter Number two had a boyfriend with whom words were exchanged late one night. She returned to her flat in tears; an hour or so later the doorbell rang and there he stood, a vodka bottle in hand, the top knocked off to make a vase and a rhododendron flower from the park set inside it. She forgave him everything with no more ado, and so she should have done.

Another friend tells a heart-throbbing story of taking her boyfriend to the airport after he had been staying with her. She drove back home, and walked into the bedroom and there on the bed he had prepared a collage of their life together for her: one of his socks, one of hers, one of his T-shirts, one of hers, a tape they had liked, two ticket stubs; any dry eyes out there now?

Of course, the whole point about romance is that you need to like and/or fancy the person proffering it, otherwise it is simply irritating. I can remember feeling nothing but nausea reading a barrage of poetry written to me by a rather intense chap; and a friend whose admirer used to bestow endless bouquets of carnations upon her, says, 'He was a pain, and anyway, he knew I didn't like carnations. I just wanted to hit him with them.'

We should perhaps draw a distinction here between romance and love: romance, someone said, is finding a bottle of champagne by the bed, and love is having your side of the bed warmed for you. Romance (said someone else) is having a surprise weekend booked for you, and love is being told about it, so you can get your hair done. Romance is having a weekend away booked for you, and love is your husband sitting you down and telling you that he's cancelled it because he realised you'd much prefer to stay at home and put your feet up.

And love does not have to go in for gestures; it is simply there. The loveliest story I heard was of a wife who decided to sort out her husband's underwear drawer. (Thus does romance lead us.) And right at the bottom of his drawer she found a very old, tattered, office phone directory. And on the back cover were written two series of numbers. Some time later, dabbing streaming eyes, she had realised that one was the phone number of her bachelor-girl flat, and the second was the time of the train he would meet to take her out for their first evening together.

Romance may make the world go round but love will stop it in its tracks.

Timothy Spall star of film and television including *Auf Wiedersehen Pet, Life is Sweet* and most recently in the successful, *Frank Stubbs Promotes*.

•

Twelve years ago I met a girl and fell truly, madly, deeply in love. It was the first time I'd been in love like this and I was very happy indeed.

However one small problem stood between me and my newfound amour. Three nights a week I was playing the leading role in The Knight of the Burning Pestle at the Aldwych Theatre, London, and for the rest of the week I was playing a leading role in a BBC Play for Today, being shot on location in the Cotswolds. The problem was that my lover lived in a council flat on the outskirts of Wolverhampton.

Physically I was dividing myself between London and the Cotswolds, while emotionally I only wanted to be in Wolverhampton.

After a couple of disastrous attempts at trying to negotiate my three locations on public transport, I decided there was only one thing to be done – purchase a motorcycle. I had been on one before, just often enough to know I shouldn't get on one again! But this was a time for throwing caution to the wind.

So I bought one off an oboe player in the BBC orchestra and, at the first opportunity, loaded the thing on to the last train to Wolverhampton after my performance at the Aldwych. On arrival, I realised I didn't know how to get from the station to my love's council flat, nor how to start the motorbike.

I got it going eventually and I gave her address to the last cabbie in the station forecourt, saying that I would follow him. My confidence grew by the mile. Soon I was conjuring this vision of yours truly astride a Honda 250cc super-dream American spec job... until the cab shot into a concealed entrance, and I jammed on the brakes, bringing me back to reality with a start.

I paid the cabbie and thanked him for his patience. The object of my mission appeared at her kitchen window, beckoning me in. I left the machine where it stood and hurried to her boudoir. Within a few minutes I realised why I had been doing such mad things to get where I was ... the rest is private.

For the next ten days I commuted from Wolverhampton to Circencester on my trusty steed. My confidence and ability as a biker did indeed grow to the point where I decided to chance the motorway (breaking the law in the process, as I only had a provisional licence). The first two journeys to Circencester on minor roads seemed to take me via Ababa Adiba. By taking the motorway I managed to cut the journey down from three and a quarter hours to just over an hour and a half. This, of course, meant more time with my love.

One morning I left Wolverhampton a bit late (again) and as I was supposed to be on the Circencester set at 7 am I had to pretend I was Barry Sheen. The scene to be shot that morning was 'a cricket match in flaming June.' Needless to say it was pissing down!

Anybody who rides a motorbike knows that without due caution and the correct attire, riding in the rain is no fun at all, and potentially very dangerous. I was wearing an ankle-length ex-army raincoat done up with one button under the chin, thin cotton trousers, and sandals with no socks. On my head I had an open-fronted helmet, old-fashioned goggles (cracked), and wrapped around my face a ladies' silk scarf, *a la* Isadora Duncan, to keep the flies out of my mouth. Nobody was going to take me for Marlon Brando in The Wild One.

Unlike Isadora, the silk scarf was not about to strangle me, but something every bit as bizarre was about to happen as I hurtled down the M5 at 90mph, drunk with love and desperate to get to my job on time.

I was OK for time, but by now it was absolutely chucking it down and I was finding it increasingly difficult to breathe. As I gasped for air I seemed to be sucking in water. The more I gasped the more water I guzzled. I began to panic, feeling faint and almost losing control of the bike. I had enough presence of mind to realise I had to stop. I pulled onto the hard shoulder where I fell off the bike and into a ditch. When I tried to remove the scarf I found that the G-force from the speed and the water had sealed it tight against my mouth and nose. For a few terrifying moments I really thought I was going to drown. At last, with one almighty tug, I managed to get it off and breathe again. I could just see the headlines in the next day's papers, 'Young actor drowns on motorbike!'

By the way, I married the lady in question three months later.

Paul McCartney, the former Beatle, singer and songwriter,
leader of WINGS, farmer and legend.

●

The night Linda and I met, I spotted her across a
crowded club, and although I normally would have
been nervous at chatting her up, I realised I had to, so,
when she passed our table I asked her to come with us to
another club. She said yes.

I realise now that if she had said no we wouldn't have
married and our four beautiful kids would not have
blessed our lives.

Pushiness worked for me that night!

Sir Ian McKellen, leading Shakespearean actor who has also
appeared in *Ian McKellen Acting Shakespeare* and on television in
*Tales of The City* and on film in *Last Action Hero*.

•

I n the autumn of 1987 I returned to London, after a
year working hard in the USA. I had been touring in
my solo show, Acting Shakespeare, hither and thither
and had earned enough dollars to take a sustained
holiday. My plan was to stay at home, find my friends
again and take time out to try and understand what I
wanted to work on next. I'd even got doubts as to whether
I wanted to carry on acting.

At a lunch party, I met up with a friend who, in my
absence, had transformed himself. When I went to
America, he had been a fast-living businessman, a restless
achiever. Now he was calm, obviously at ease with his new
life. He had given up his share of the business and was
working, almost full-time, as a volunteer for London
Lighthouse.

He was radiant as he described the new centre devoted
to people with HIV and AIDS, helping them and their
families to cope with their desperately changed
circumstances.

An abandoned school in Notting Hill Gate was being
rebuilt to provide meeting-rooms for counselling, with a
cafe and garden at the back and a residential floor on top
with 26 beds where the sick could recuperate and the
dying rest in peace.

What a vision! And what a transformation it had inspired in my friend.

The building was being financed in part by a Government Grant – after all some might think the volunteers were doing the work of the National Health Service. But when I heard about it all, disaster was imminent. The public money was late in arriving and Christopher Spence, Director of London Lighthouse, was about to send the builders home with no certainty that he would ever be able to afford to bring them back.

So that's how I came to do Acting Shakespeare for 10 weeks at the Playhouse in London's West End. I've never known a show organised with so little trouble. The idea was simple. We would tell the audiences that every penny (minus VAT) would go intact to the Lighthouse, where their donations would be transformed overnight into bricks and mortar for one of the most imaginative new buildings in London.

The Playhouse scarcely charged us rent even though it was agreed that their staff should be paid. A philanthropist underwrote the inevitable costs of publicity.

After each performance, I bullied my willing audiences to fill the red buckets, which I and Lighthouse volunteers held out in the theatre foyer. Over the three months, we raised about £½ million. No sooner was that achieved, than the Government's money came through, with an extra £¾ million as 'London Lighthouse has captured the public's imagination'.

I had my own reward. In the middle of the run, as I was holding the bucket in the lobby, an acquaintance told me about Section 28. This was a nasty, brutish measure, intended to inhibit local authorities from subsidising lesbian and gay groups. In future it was to be illegal for them to 'promote homosexuality'.

Another cause: another emergency. Before I knew it, I was helping; and, effortlessly, after 49 years of equivocation, I came out and said to anyone who was interested (and many who weren't) that I was gay. Since when, *my* life was transformed – but that's another story.

Wendy Perriam, best selling novelist whose books include *Born of Woman*, *The Stillness the Dancing*, *Sin City*. She is currently working on her eleventh novel.

•

Most of my great love affairs have been, alas, tragically unrequited. I suspect it's my own fault for choosing curs and bastards. But just *one* relationship – with a genuine cur and bastard – was ecstatically mutual. It was love at first sight – no doubt about it. As the sicky, trembly scrap of a puppy fixed me with his Bournville eyes, I too went wobbly at the knees, flung myself upon him and covered him with hot wet kisses, instantly reciprocated. We spent an uncoventional first night together – he under the bed, me *in* it – but by dawn he was on top of me; I relishing his warm and sensuous weight.

I named him William, after William Rufus, since he was both regal and red – an Irish setter, with an Irish temperament to match – volatile, passionate, neurotic, unreliable, and with those smiling Irish eyes.

I remember our first row – he wolfed a large elaborate birthday cake I had made (and iced) for a ninety-year-old aunt, and later sicked it up in my study on the proofs of my latest novel. He also ate my black fishnet tights and, over the years, several dozen toilet-rolls. Though actually, personal hygiene was never his strong point, as he had an incorrigible tendency to roll in things unspeakable. Fortunately, I was well-practised in washing muddy

87

sports kit (my first husband was a rugby fiend), which stood me in good stead when it came to washing canines. The bath-tub would end up full of grit and hairs, the bathroom semi-flooded, but – oh! – how handsome William looked once I'd burnished his coat with henna and bay rum, and spent long hours with the hair dryer.

Sometimes, he misunderstood the purpose of all this titivation, assuming it was for the benefit of other, rival females. And what bitter pangs of jealousy I suffered when he sluck off with some lucky bitch, or spent the night with his current bit of fluff, sidling back next morning with a truly hangdog look. But I hadn't the heart to stay sour when he pressed his nose so passionately into my groin, or left love-offerings on my bed: a soggy half-chewed slipper, or the most precious and malodorous of his bones. And anyway I knew, deep down, that I had never been so idolized in any previous relationship. What other male would follow me all round the house, sit on my foot while I worked, and gaze at me adoringly, or greet me at the front door with an impassioned aria of top-C barks and yelps, when I'd only popped out to the post-box?

So when he finally died (an event so tragic it is best passed over in grim black-bordered silence), I knew I had to make some recompense for all he had given me, pour out my appreciation for a lifetime of devotion. His funeral, I decided, would be a genuine labour of love – no expense nor effect spared.

My second husband (a woodwork fiend) set about crafting his coffin – none of your cheap whitewood, but finest-grain mahogany, with real brass handles, and lined with a magnificent velvet curtain in Tyrian purple. His shroud was my best Harrods dressing-gown – a Chinese silk creation, printed with peacocks: symbol of both love and immortality. We filled his coffin with grave-goods, in the manner of Tutankhamen, to prepare him for the Other Side – a big fat juicy marrowbone, chicken breast in jelly, chocolate Doggy Drops, I composed a funeral ode, an elegy modelled on those of Catullus, with overtones of Shelley's 'Adonais', and agonized about the choice of requiem. Would Verdi's be too theatrical, Fauré's too emotionally intense?

On a dark day in November, the funeral guests assembled in our garden – my parents, our three children, the neighbours from both sides, and assorted friends and relatives. My daughters laid the wreath – red roses, again for love, entwined with evergreens to represent the everlasting vigour of that love. My stepson was in charge of the cassette (we'd settled on the Verdi) and soon the strains of the 'Dies Irae' were thundering over the privet hedge. When I rose to deliver the funeral address, solemnizing William's official passing to the Great Lamp-Post In The Sky, there was not a dry eye in the house.

The obsequies over, I served tea and Spiller's Shapes (spread liberally with Pedigree Chum), and we talked fondly about the Dear Departed, recalling the high spots of his life: the time he jumped off Teddington Bridge in pursuit of a black swan; his Tuesday-evening Obedience Classes (he restricted obedience thenceforward to Tuesdays, after dusk); the embarrassing occasion when he cocked his leg over the vicar's calf-skin shoe.

Once the guests had departed, my husband crept back to the now moonlit garden to fill in the grave and plant a weeping willow – weeping himself beneath the mournful moon.

A fortnight later, I attended the cremation of another

nonagenarian aunt. The coffin looked like chipboard; a vase of plastic lilies stood on the so-called altar, and there was no address or ode; only two wavering low-key hymns accompanied by a bronchitic organ. As I watched the cheapskate coffin glide away behind tatty Dralon curtains in a startling shade of electric blue, I whispered to my husband, there and then, would he please order more mahogany and sharpen up his saw. I had decided to be buried in the garden – not in any soulless crematorium – so that I could be beside my Beloved for all eternity.

R.I.P

**Freddie Cooke, Managing Director of Porter Cooke Executive Relations, a committed believer in all things British and an enthusiastic supporter of ROC.**

•

I married for love – too early.
We had two sons for love – too early then, but great now.

I joined the Royal Air Force for love – of my country – old fashioned, but true.

I run conferences to 'talk up Britain' – for love of my country and proud to say it.

I help with charities for love – of your fellow men and women – help where you can.

I support blindly, the English Rugby, Cricket and Football teams – that has to be for love!

On reflection, I realise that I have probably done everything important in my life for love… and I would probably do it all again.

But next time I'll make some money!!

Rick Holmes is an advertising consultant and director of a
design company and spare time humorous writer.

•

This is a true story of events that took place in the
king-size marital bed, and later on the carpet at the
bottom of the stairs one night, or rather early one morning, in April 1981. Just an ordinary tale of how I, unwill-
ingly, came to do something for which others have been
prosecuted – that is, delivering my own child.

My wife was pregnant and three days past her delivery
date. She appeared to be doing it all by the book, having
survived the initial alarm of a threatened miscarriage
when she was shopping in Birmingham (brought on, no
doubt by being informed how far she was overdrawn on
her Barclaycard).

It was our second child; two-year-old Matthew had
been told that Mummy was growing a brother or sister for
him in her tummy. Matthew clearly thought this was a
silly process since it obviously caused Mummy so much
inconvenience. No doubt he felt it would be easier to do it
in the garden where he knew, even at two-and-a-half,
most things were grown. My wife, being heavily but not
obsessively into doing things as naturally as possible, was
quietly confident of her ability to direct proceedings
successfully, second time around.

Matthew had been induced, care of the West London
Hospital, 12 days late but without epidurals, drugs, gas or

any other support system designed to reinforce a mothers's natural determination to populate the planet.

Father, the night before the great event, had not been in the best of moods having lost a client from his advertising business. In a fruitless attempt to restore humour to life, considerable quantities of good malt whisky had been consumed with the inevitable result that spirits had dampened the excitement of the imminent birth. Wife, wisely not wishing to witness husband's assault upon the Scottish distilleries, had retired early. Husband finally collapsed in a haze of evil fumes beside her around midnight, hoping not quite for death, but at least for an escape from the problems of the world for several heavy slumbering hours.

But it was not to be.

At 1.30am wife, discovering she's having contractions every five minutes, sits bolt upright. This comes as a surprise, since the previous afternoon the hospital had informed her that they'd see her again in a week. But then, as mothers know, no pregnancy is the same – even midwives get caught short in the supermarket.

Suddenly, The Flood. Wife's waters break and occupants of the bed abandon ship in disorder. As if in one of those fast-forward films, coats and bags are assembled, clothes thrown on, son is dressed and strapped, half-asleep, into his seat in the back of the car while the team prepare for a trip to the hospital two miles up the road.

Wife remains calm, believing time is on her side. Husband is already massively hung over and concerned only that his general condition may not be strictly within the legal limit for driving. Wife is looking particularly fetching in her nightie, leather boots and over-coat. In full motherly splendour, hands protectively in classic pose hanging on to the bulge, she starts to go down the stairs.

Alas, at approximately the eighth stair out of 14 she realises that she feels extraordinarily uncomfortable. Slow progress down the remaining stairs ends with her squatting on the bottom step. Remaining perfectly calm, she informs husband the trip to hospital is, she believes, about to become superfluous. Husband, behaving like a horde of maniacs under the influence of Newcastle Brown, attempts to dial 999.

Husband returns to the hot seat – the bottom of the stairs. Inspection by both parties reveals the interesting sight, not surprising in the circumstances, of a baby's head intent on being followed by the rest of said child. Wife has the presence of mind to demand towels from the kitchen. Husband's hangover miraculously disappears as he realises he had no option but to get seriously involved. Luckily, he is not in the least bit squeamish.

Wife, however, has now, so-to-speak, got the bit between her teeth and decided to sort all this out. There are no complications and a series of magnificent pushes that would do justice to the front row of the Wigan Rugby League Football first-team result in a small person being almost literally fired into husband's hands like a human cannon ball.

The new arrival announces its appearance with surprising vocal power. Having checked gender and that all bits are attached and working (relief!), helpless-looking husband enquires what on earth he should do next. Nature, of course, has provided the perfect solution and wife indicates the correct position. Within seconds, Anna Louise is locked on to left breast more securely than a space shuttle in a docking manoeuvre.

All is quiet, save for a contented sucking sound as the

ambulance team, true to within a minute of their promise, storm the front door SAS-style. Reassured all is under control, they offer congratulations and send for a midwife to mop up.

Husband suddenly remembers son stranded in the car. Matthew, initially fascinated by flashing lights and ambulances, is now only interested in the present which I tell him is waiting for him upstairs. Clambering past mother and daughter with me, Matthew asks what is it that's stuck to Mummy. I inform him it's his new sister.

Much later, when wife has been taken to hospital for a check-up, I ring my office to tell them I've got a daughter. They're delighted. I then proudly inform them that I delivered her myself. My secretary listens politely and then tells me to stop playing the fool. I am momentarily at a loss for words until I realise it's 1st April. Later, when the truth is confirmed and the champagne starts flowing, people start dropping in and gathering at the bottom of the stairs to gaze at where X marks the spot – the scene of the action which, miraculously, did not seen to suffer too much wear and tear.

Rolf Harris, Australian singer, TV star and artist whose hit
songs include *Two Little Boys*, *Jake the Peg*, and
*Stairway to Heaven*.

•

On a recent tour of Australia I was missing my wife
Alwen back in England. I felt I had to do something
to bring us closer together otherwise I'd go crazy, not
seeing her for weeks on end.

I bought a piece of raw jade and spent the next six
weeks carving and polishing it into a pendant.

I guess I must have driven the musicians on the tour
barmy because every time they found me I was beavering
at this thing.

However I found it excellent therapy for the pain of
separation.

**Barry Porter, MP for Wirral South, a director of Porter Cooke,
a rugby union enthusiast and much appreciated as one
of ROC's patrons.**

●

'Love is the sweetest thing'. So says Al Bowlly who was a better singer than Bing Crosby or Frank Sinatra. Who said that? I did! Unfortunately Mr Bowlly was blitzed by the Luftwaffe in 1942 at the Cafe de Paris. Whether he was singing about love at the time is not recorded, but I think is it fair to say that he died for love. I have not done that – so far!

What I did for love is perhaps an activity shared by many middle aged dreamers and practitioners of self delusion. I played rugby for love. Not, I hasten to add, the rugby of Will Carling and Jeremy Guscott or the rugby of Twickenham and Murrayfield. I played the rugby of the municipal park on the remote uncut field, plentifully manured by the cows and the sheep. Spectators were an extinct species and to some extent so were the players. Carling and Guscott are used to playing in teams of 15 players and for 80 minutes. This would have caused cardiac arrest for the bulk of the overweight tubercular participants in the Extra V 15 (normally about 12 turned up).

About 20 minutes each way was what we could manage under vague rules invented by a myopic referee of indeterminate age and doubtful sanity. It always rained, it was always cold, we always lost.

On reflection, I didn't love that part. It was the bit when after a tepid bath in liquid mud we indulged in half a gallon of lukewarm, flat bitter that I enjoyed. Thus emboldened we actually believed that we had been Carling and Guscott. We had a faith worthy of fundamental Islam that we had executed a side step despite the evidence that it was physically impossible.

I loved the dreams. I loved the illusion that next week I would be Carling. I actually believed that the shortness of breath, the arthritis of the knee and the continual nausea would magically disappear.

Reality never overcame the pathetic and ridiculous belief I had in myself. In one way it was narcissistic except that Narcissus was a young and beautiful boy which I have to concede I am not and indeed never was.

But, there is nothing wrong with a dream or the love of a dream. The facts of life are very often too horrible to contemplate, the illusions are worthy of affection. That is what I did for love.

I haven't for obvious reasons been able to discuss these matters with the deceased Mr Bowlly, but I am sure he would have approved. 'Love is the sweetest thing'.

Jane Reed, former editor of *Woman*, *Womans Own* and managing editor of *Today*, is Director of Corporate Affairs at News International, Rupert Murdoch's publishing arm in the UK.

•

I had been on the magazine three weeks when they announced the closure. Tips and wrinkles for the servant classes were not called for in the just-about-to-swing sixties. Grudgingly I accepted a job on *Honey*, a monthly billed as the first glossy magazine for teenagers. The launch issue had bombed and everyone knew it was unlikely to go to issue four. But any port in a storm.

The new, post-launch editor who interviewed me was heavily pregnant and somewhat underwhelming. Not exactly a teenager, I thought. What does she know?

What did I know? This was Audrey Slaughter who became arguably the most influential editor in the young women's magazine market of the 60's and 70's. A kind of Miss Jean Brodie for a whole gaggle of journalists most of whom made it to dizzy heights later on – from Janet Street-Porter to Eve Pollard, Frankie McGowan to Maggie Goodman.

Was it luck or talent on Audrey's part? As in life, probably a bit of both, but 'her girls' loved and feared her during the most formative years of our working lives. She gave us responsibility beyond our experience and fought for us and the magazine against closure and censure.

She taught me many things. As I deliberated over convoluted cover lines she would ask: What are you trying to say? I'd tell her and she'd snap, well why don't you say it then?

Her guiding principle in magazine editing seemed to be that there is no such word as 'can't'. We turned somersaults for her in every issue. We embarassed ourselves and other victims daily in words and pictures; we had miniscule editorial budgets so WE were the models. We and our families and friends were the subjects in the real-life and beauty features. We would do anything for her.

We took the whole magazine on the road to Liverpool pre-empting Beatlemania, to Sheffield, to Bristol. We set up a vast chain of 'Honey boutiques' in stuffy old stores up and down Britain. The magazine flourished, became the centre of the swinging sixties, and we celebrated. With parties. Very big and ambitious parties on very small budgets.

One such – and you really would only do this for someone you were in awe of – was the Honey Ball, a South Sea Island extravaganza in the summer of '63.

I assume the directors had refused to subsidise this latest adventure, so Audrey decided that this party was to be in the Fleetway House Canteen in downtown Farringdon Street, and that tickets would be £10, a lot in those days. 'For charity,' Audrey announced.

A large, dank, subterranean space with no charm, the canteen smelled faintly of chip fat and cold cabbage. The moment I had said 'But Audrey you caaaaan't,' I knew there was no turning back.

The guest list read like the membership of the Ad Lib (the Langans of its day): Michael Caine, Terence Stamp, The Beatles and their modely and actressy girlfriends, and so on through hot names of the day, many of whom have since cooled to extinction.

I had been on holiday during the crucial planning period and returned to find that Audrey had got away with murder. She was in her expansive impresario mode. To set the scene, she had decided that on arrival we would take the guests on a 'journey of a lifetime through the tropical glades of somewhere in the Pacific'.

This was to be done by 'whizzing' all the guests up to the sixth floor and down to the basement in the Fleetway House lifts. During this exotic journey, the hostesses (pale, plump me and a stick insect from the postroom in sarongs and leis) would entertain the guests with South Sea Island music played on a portable tape recorder (there being no sound systems in those days) hidden behind the office pot plant and some cut-out palm trees in the grubby corner of the lift.

I wonder if Michael Caine remembers it? I do. With more horror than a roomful of spiders. Imagine being stuck in the lift with Michael Caine for fifteen minutes with this script: 'Welcome to your holiday of a lifetime'; (wait for jet take-off noises from the scratchy little tape): '…where you will be entertained by dusky maidens and eat the food of the gods.' (wait for squeaky music to a background of sea breaking on a shore). 'Fasten your seat belts, we are about to land in Paradise.' (Exit).

Unfortunately the lifts were very slow and very noisy. And the script was rather short. I smiled ingratiatingly at Michael Caine and the starlet on his arm in the long breaks between the dialogue. They looked at me in total bewilderment. What were they doing here? Terry Stamp, as I recall, flatly refused to get in the lift and legged it down the stairs before anyone could stop him.

The whole process of receiving each guest took up to fifteen minutes. Ground hostesses were refusing people entry unless they did the lift thing. Guests were literally beating down the lift doors to get out.

When the hundred and fiftieth person had asked wearily why they had to go up six floors and down seven to get to the ball, all I could say was: because the Editor says so.

Once in the basement, the institution green canteen had been transformed into a palm fringed beach of sand. Guests were required to crunch their way over to the self service area where Mrs Hughes, wife of the House Manager, was serving her food of the gods, a special 'Hawiian Rice' dish. This was 90% rice and 10% mixed veg. and pineapple pieces.

For inexplicable reasons many more people turned up than were expected and so the last 50 uncomplainingly received a spoonful of plain rice (without the Hawiian) on a paper plate. One or two of the less famous (staff relatives and the like) did complain and said they wanted their money back. We rounded them up and put them in charge of the showbiz editor who made them all feel important by interviewing them for what he said would eventually be a feature. In their dreams.

A nightmare was emerging in front of me. The sparkling wine had run out. No more pineapple. No one could dance on the sand.

What saved the day were the guests. The trendy young stars and celebrities table-hopped from one corner of the 'South Sea Island' to another, delighted to be seen with their celebrated equals. The dusky maidens simply watched, fascinated.

The cabaret was The Dave Clark Five and they were

innocent and happy. A few names jammed with the group and suddenly, in spite of the limp paper palm trees, the plastic cutlery, and the lack of food and drink the canteen was jumping.

It was at this point that Mrs Hughes said fire regulations meant we had to vacate the building by eleven. "But we have the Beatles here", I shrieked. She was unmoved. Out. All out.

Looking back I don't see Audrey actually being there. Things like migraines would often excuse her from her greater excesses. If she was there she was probably flirting outrageously with someone under a paper palm tree.

When I told this story to her many decades later she had absolutely no recollection of it at all. But she laughed until she cried. I stayed with her for almost another two years until I heard she was going to give another party....

George Baker, actor in numerous productions played the title role in the highly successful *Wexford Files*. He is currently working on his own scripts.

•

What I did for love begs many questions. The greatest of these is 'what is love?' Love, poor damaged word, used to persuade the reluctant to respond.

'I love you, don't I?' 'I love you, Gwyneth.' 'Oh, Dai. Here you hold the bible, I'll take them down myself.'

The love of country for which men are prepared to die and take their brothers with them.

The love of air, rain and the forest, which is a joke among men.

Infinite Love, an archaic concept but, 'I know that my redeemer liveth...'

Love, a blessed word full of laughter, understanding and friendship. The foundation on which lasting relationships are built.

I first properly understood the word when I was watching with my wife and she was dying of cancer; it is a word made up of spirit, courage, joy, acceptance of universal thought and, above all laughter.

What did I do for love? I watched with wonder, I live to emulate and laugh because 'love casteth out fear'.

Heidi Kingstone, Canadian journalist, former staff writer on *The Daily Mail* and *Today*, contributes to national newspapers and magazines and is researching her first book.

•

Maybe, it was the smell of manure. But I doubt it. Although you never know. But something got me going to the back stretch of the Toronto track to hang out by the paddock trying to catch the attention of a five foot three inch, one hundred and ten pound, blond-haired, angel-faced jockey. Oh God, it's true, I was having a Damon Runyon crisis.

Along with my friend Paddy we certainly managed to catch the attention of some of the other even less salubrious characters. Dressed, in retrospect, like two giant bumblebees (this was a long long time ago), we wore black and yellow striped tops, black pedal pushers and high heeled yellow mules. Trainer and jockey Adolph and Hugo were stung by this 'package deal'. It was not to bee.

Instead, by stealthy investigation, I sussed out Joey's home address and nightly, Paddy and I in the Audi, drove the twenty miles to deepest, darkest suburban Mississauga to gaze up at his forty-seventh floor high-rise window. Or just as often to the dank, deserted track to tread on earth perhaps touched by him.

With similar cunning I discovered a friend of his sister's, a beautician who, after much persuading, set up a blind date. I had hung around the two dollar wicket long enough.

111

Armed with a tape of Gene Pitney wailing out 'I was only 24 hours from Tulsa', I hit the highway to rendez-vous with my beleaguered in Niagara Falls. A place so grim a nuclear explosion couldn't expunge its memory from the earth. Still, the mid-Canadian suburbanality looked lovely in the mist to me.

There on my big date, I got dinner at the revolving Skylon restaurant atop one of Niagara's hottest tourist attractions, where you can get your picture taken in a barrel pretending to go over the Falls. For someone who considers Claridges just this side of provincial, I can only think my mules were too tight.

Joey was racing at the B-track in Fort Erie, a few miles shy of the American border. I never made it into the winners' circle and I gather neither did he. I also never saw him again.

Naim Attallah, owner of Quartet Books, his own books include *Women, Singular Encounters, Of A Certain Age* and most recently *More Of A Certain Age*.

●

In 1971 I gave up a lucrative career in banking to start up on my own. It was a hazardous decision because I had a wife and young son who were totally dependant on me and my ability to succeed.

At the time we lived in London in Sloane Street at the junction of Pont Street. The rent was affordable while I had a regular income, but when I sacrificed security for independence it soon became difficult to make ends meet.

However, it was imperative to survive. I was determined not to look back; the prospect of abandoning ship and starting to look for another 'safe' nine-to-five job was just too dispiriting. I buried myself in work, accepting anything I was offered to keep body and soul together. I travelled extensively in search of business opportunites, unwavering in my determination to be architect of my own destiny.

The predictable result of my new frenetic lifestyle was a huge increase in stress which in turn commuted a moderate liking for tobacco into an uncontrollable addiction. My new independent world was filtered through a cloud of exhaled smoke. My eyes sank into their sockets and my complexion turned a sickly yellowish ochre.

Most nights when I was in London I used to run out of cigarettes (stockpiling supplies would have made it difficult not to acknowledge the addiction), and if it was late at night and the shops were closed the concierge at the nearby Carlton Tower Hotel would obligingly find me a packet of my favourite brand. My enslavement to the weed was total.

One such night my wife pointed out the absurdity of working so hard for a future which I was simultaneously jeopardising by my noxious habit. If I really cared for her and our future I would surely give up, she said. Her words cut through the smoke-filled room and pierced my poor defences. Are we responsible only for ourselves in this life or are we also responsible for those whom we love and cherish? The answer was painfully clear.

Like most smokers I had of course made sporadic attempts to give up smoking, with varying degrees of success, always reverting to the habit. This time it was different. My wife had touched a raw nerve; she had brought my love for her into question, and that was more than I could endure. With the frenzy of a Road to Damascus convert I hurled the packet of cigarettes (fresh from the concierge) out of the window. I never smoked again.

Since that day I have often reflected that love is the most powerful motivating force. Nothing else would have made me confront my addiction so starkly. Nothing else matters quite so much.

Pushpa Sellers, Indian born writer who has contributed to two anthologies, *Sleeping Rough* and *The Likes of Us* She has just completed her first novel.

•

It was going to be a registry office wedding, just two close friends as witnesses, no bridal gown, no guests and definitely no family. After all the opposition from his parents and mine we were determined that this was the only way.

I had been diagnosed as having SLE (Lupus) an auto-immune disease five months previous to this; one of the major reasons that his parents thought it was unwise to marry. There seemed to be too many imponderables. He was unemployed and I was ill.

The night before the wedding, my leg, which had been swollen, got worse. We went to the casualty ward where the doctor told us that it was a blood clot which was potentially lethal.

'As I see it', the doctor said, 'you've got two choices; either you postpone the wedding or I can give you an injection, if you promise to come back in five hours so we can put you on a drip.' With that he left us on our own to decide.

'Maybe God's trying to tell us that we're making a mistake.' I sobbed.

'No', J said, kissing my hand gently, 'He's telling us that you need someone to look after you.'

We *did* get married the next day and five hours later I was back in hospital to have the blood clot removed.

We're still happily married after sixteen years and he still looks after me.

George Melly, musician, singer writer, critic, art lecturer and voice over, he is author of more than a dozen books including *Rum, Bum and Concertina* and *Mellymobile*.

•

In the 1950s I was a singer with a jazz band and travelled about the country in an unreliable van staying at the cheapest digs we were able to find. I had a certain reputation among fans but my life, while lively enough, was by no means luxurious. Then the *Daily Express*, Manchester edition, decided to put on a travelling variety show called 'Rhythm with the Stars' and not only was the band I sang with part of the bill, I was booked as compere for the entire venture.

Among the other acts was a glamorous young woman whom I shall call X, then famous as a cabaret artiste and tired businessman's dream. My sex life at that time was varied and full, but it certainly didn't include people like her. I was surprised therefore that during the run of the show she took me under her wing, despite considerable opposition from her manager, a formidable woman who clearly disapproved of our liaison. I was still more surprised when, on the very last night of the show, she invited me into her bed.

The next day we all went our various ways and to be frank I didn't expect to hear from her again. Then that evening when we were appearing in a small corn-exchange in Norfolk, the manager approached me with an air of surpressed excitement and awe, to tell me that X was on the telephone. X told me that she had to see me again – was desperate to see me again – and was it possible that I could make it up to Sheffied the following week where she was appearing in variety?

Naturally, although I could ill afford it, I went up there at the first opportunity, only to be told by her manager that X had a bad headache and couldn't see me. I returned to London in quite a bad temper but had no sooner entered my flat than she was on the phone again explaining that she really had had a terrible migraine and could I *please* come to Cardiff on the following Monday. I did, only to be told, yet again, that she must have dinner with her agent and our meeting was impossible.

This time I made up my mind not to listen to her any more, but a long and loving telephone conversation with her and a promise that this time it would be different and that anyway her next engagement was in Brighton helped to change my mind.

I went down to Brighton only to find that this time, yes she would see me and yes she intended to take me out to dinner, but I would not be alone. Three other previous boyfriends had turned up all equally convinced that this was *the* night.

I had a bit of a go at X's secretary; how it was obviously she who manipulated my love, refused me entry to the dressing room and had now played this last malicious trick!

She looked at me sadly. 'You could be blaming the wrong person' she said.

With the other suitors I made my way to a public house and got to be rather drunk.

X did take us out to dinner although I have little

recollection of it, and no idea how I came to wake up on the sofa of a hotel on the front, and was forced on regaining consciousness to battle through a gale to the station to catch the first train. I heard no more.

Some years later, however, I mentioned this incident to someone else in the profession and they said X was famous for going to bed with people once and then having them run around all over the country at her invitation only to discover her entirely unavailable.

She is dead now, but I happened to see her (although I didn't recognise her) in a restaurant a year or two ago. She greeted me. She had grown to be very fat but was extremely friendly and by this time I couldn't really imagine my anguish some 40 years before. At least I've never forgotten her and realise that what I did for love, while genuine at the time, makes me look a total idiot.

Richard Barber, journalist and writer, former editor of *Woman* and *TV Times* he now contributes regularly to *GMTV* and magazines.

•

The faintly ludicrous way I earn my living is by interviewing celebrities – actors, authors, pop singers – for newspapers and magazines. They are, by turn, funny, dull, fascinating, self-obsessed and very often very rich.

They are also different from you and me because they are famous, and seductive, corrupting fame imposes its own unique pressures. But, as any London cabbie will tell you, we all come into and out of the world the same way which is very nearly true and something of which I try to remind myself when a particular celebrity is being particularly difficult.

Take the famous in love. Success and wealth may dictate they play the game a little differently but, in the end, love is the great leveller. Helen Mirren is a case in point. The woman once dubbed (to her extreme embarrassment) The Sex Queen of the Royal Shakespeare Company had few rivals in her generation of gifted stage actresses. She has since enjoyed considerable success playing the uncompromising Jane Tennison in Granada Television's *Prime Suspect*. But, at bedrock, she is a theatre actress.

Yet we met in Los Angeles – not a town noted for its strong theatrical tradition – because that is where she lives. And no, she isn't there, either, because she's about to become an international film star (although she's appeared in a fair few). The fiercely independent Helen Mirren is there because of love.

The lucky man is American director Taylor (*An Officer and A Gentleman*) Hackford and the moment she met him, she says, her fate was sealed. 'It's funny, isn't it? But sometimes you do end up getting what you want. I was ready for Taylor. I'd dedicated my whole life up until that point to my work. Anyone who came along fitted in – or didn't. Work came first.'

Now the position is reversed and it has produced the most exquisite dilemma. 'I get so scared,' she says. 'That I'm losing my professional grip, my position in the world of British theatre. You've got to be in it to win it, so to speak. You've got to be seen. You've got to do the important work. You can't just dip in and out.

'It's the most terrible tug. If I were to do the sustained body of work I should do, to remind people in Britain I am primarily a theatre actress, that could be disastrous for my relationship with Taylor. I've turned down any number of jobs because they would have meant our being apart too long.'

Helen Mirren would no doubt envy the solution of rock singer Jon Bon Jovi, the much-fancied, fabulously wealthy rock singer who now has just the two women in his life – his wife, Dorothea, and their new daughter, Stevie Rose. 'I can rock with the best of them,' says Jon. 'But I sure am happy with these two women. Every man should be as lucky as I am.'

And every man, he says, should do what he's doing: taking his wife and child on the road with him. 'I'm blessed tenfold because the two of them can go to work with me.' Fine. But this deep-seated contentment with marriage and fatherhood is scarcely the stuff of hard-drinking, loose rock stardom.

Jon Bon Jovi is having none of it. 'That's stereotyping,' he says. 'That's judging the book by its cover. I don't hide the fact I have a wife and daughter. Actually, I'm pretty proud of them. And, if you look around – from Bono to Bruce – they're all married, they've all got kids. You can't live your life on television or on vinyl. You've got to be able to enjoy the real things away from the spotlight.'

It's a problem Michael Caine never thought he'd have to encounter. The idea, he says now, that he might one day become an actor was as foreign to him as the notion you could train at an academy for the dramatic arts. Indeed, the only reason he presented himself one day in his mid-teens at a youth club in the Walworth Road was a girl called Amy Hood.

'I didn't enrol for the drama class,' says Caine, 'because I wanted to act. I enrolled because I had a terrible teenage crush. I knew that in some scenes of most plays someone got to kiss the girl. But she was always the lead and I only ever got small parts. So you could say I became an actor to kiss a beautiful girl but failed in my ambition – and look where it got me.'

The rest, as they say, is history, including a long and famously faithful marriage in an industry where silver wedding ceremonies are not exactly thick on the ground.

Impossible to know for certain whether Kenneth Branagh and Emma Thompson will be celebrating theirs in twentysomething years from now. But it seems pretty likely. The Golden Couple of theatre, films – pretty much any art form you are to mention, in fact – look set fair for a long and happy marriage.

But it scares the daylights out of Branagh, he says, even to speculate on it. 'I'm quite prepared to accept,' he says, 'that people are interested and want to write and read about my private life. But I feel sort of superstitious about it. You can talk things away.

'It's such a personal thing, something I feel I want to resist discussing. I resist it when I see those articles in newspapers or magazines where a couple talk about how much in love they are. I don't want to be told. Those things are so private, so precious. It's like giving away gold.'

Spoken like a good 'un. But thank heavens he's in so small a minority – from a celebrity interviewer's standpoint, that is.

David Hamilton, radio and television DJ has, in the last twenty
five years, helped raise over three million pounds for charity
as a member of the showbiz eleven football team.

•

I first fell in love at 15 while I was on a family caravan
holiday in Walton-on-the-Naze. One wet afternoon I
amused myself by driving around on the dodgem cars.
Business was very quiet and the only other driver was a
very attractive girl at least a year older than me (which
seemed a lot then!). We literally bumped into each other!

One thing led to another and later that week I discovered the joys of the birds and the bees on the clifftop at
Walton-on-the-Naze.

I returned home a lovesick teenager. I lost my appetite
and even my interest in football, which normally dominated my every waking moment. After a couple of weeks
I arranged to visit my first girlfriend and cycled the long
journey from my family home in Wimbledon to her's in
Waltham Cross on the other side of London.

Sadly when I got there I discovered all the magic had
gone. The electricity that existed between us on the
clifftops had blown a fuse.

At the tender age of 15 I learned the terrible truth
about holiday romances – they seldom survive the
journey home.

Bob Payton, American hospitality impresario, founder of the
*Chigaco Pizza Pie Factory*, TV and radio broadcaster who
owns twenty six restaurants throughout Europe.

•

The first time I met Wendy, my wife, was when she
came to eat at one of my restaurants, the Chicago
Ribshack. She was with some mutual friends and they sat
at table 13. I guess we fell in love that night.

I was building a new restaurant in Charing Cross Road,
'Payton Place', at the time, and I invited her to come and
have a look at it the following day. We had our picture
taken together in front of a hoarding which bore the
legend, 'The shrimp boats are coming, but the men are
bringing back the crabs.'

That night we went to Langan's and I wore a dinner
jacket to impress her. But I was involved with someone
else and Wendy was headed back to Chicago.

Two years later I was in Chicago on business and I
called Wendy to ask her out for dinner. I didn't announce
myself, I simply said 'The shrimp boats are coming, but
the men are bringing back the crabs,' like it was a secret
code between us.

She said she couldn't go out with me because she was
meeting someone else for dinner.

So I found out where they were dining and I called the
restaurant in the middle of the evening and asked to
speak to Mrs Becker (Wendy). When she came to the

phone I said, 'Mrs Becker, you house is on fire, you're going to have to leave the restaurant immediately.'

Of course she recognized my voice and I guess she also recognized that I would go to any lengths to distract her from another man's attentions.

Angela Neustatter journalist and writer contributes regularly to *The Guardian* and *The Independent*. Her books include *Hyenas in Petticoats*. She is currently researching a book on age.

•

The beginning was, for me, pure unadulterated love. It was all those over the top, silly, sentimental cliches rolled into one, as I gazed in loving amazement at the unimaginably tiny person cradled in my arms, flesh of my flesh, the stunning answer to nine months of unanswerable questions. What I did not stop to contemplate in the sheer, self-indulgent delight of those first magnificent days of motherhood was the grand scale implications of being mother to a son.

Not seeing myself as a Jocasta or Gertrude, not having the dominant and desperate ways of history and mythology's matriarchs uppermost in my mind, as I cradled the tiny first-born son to my breast and felt his fingers splayed across my skin, watched as his body became plumper, his face spread into clownish early smiles, I did not stop and take stock of the fact that as a mother you are the first woman with whom a boy experiences love. Or that I was the woman from whom he must first learn about separation and the anguished feelings which may go with that necessary pulling apart. Adam Jukes in his fascinating book 'Why Men Hate Women' (Free Association Press) explores the way men, who have not been able to separate satisfactorily from mothers, act out their ambivalent feelings later in life. For better or for worse, this mother-son relationship will provide the original intimate knowledge of the opposite sex which the boy will carry with him through life.

It was realisation which occurred when Zek, this first born son, was little over a year old. He was a highly emotional child, one minute all embraces, his velvety face pressed against mine or his father's as he snuggled on to a lap for a cuddle, the next a fireball of rage, protesting at some forbidden desire. On one such occasion he finished screaming, got up off the floor and just stood looking at me, very composed, an expression on his face of pure hostility.

It was a moment of reckoning, the moment in which I knew the umbilical cord had been given its first major wrench. There was no mistaking my son's separateness from me, the fact that this little person with his soft blonde curls, his fragile limbs, was stating his right to be an individual. He was pitched against me, letting me know that he did not think I was the best thing since mashed bananas just because I was Mum, and in that stance there was an unmistakable sense of the male female frisson.

The realisation was a shock but also a watershed because it forced me to drop the virtuous, self-sacrificing, all-indulging mother role I was rather enjoying and which I felt guaranteed me my son's unconditional love ad infinitum, and to contemplate what, as a mother, I thought I should bring to the life of this young male.

A good starting point seemed to be the way a son comes to view his mother, for this clearly is going to influence the way he will see other women in his life. Clearly for a contemporary mother who has absorbed the messages of feminism, the point is to avoid being regarded as the classical mother described in Adrienne Rich's 'Of Women Born' (Virago): 'As her sons have seen her the Mother in patriarchy; controlling, erotic, castrating, heart-suffering, guilt-ridden and guilt-provoking; a marble brow, a huge breast, an avid cave between her legs, snakes, swamp grass, or teeth; on her lap a helpless infant or a martyred son. She exists for one purpose; to bear and nourish the son.'

Along with many women, I have not wished to be seen by my male offspring as no more than the provider of the means of survival, comfort and support. Rather I have wanted him to view me as someone who loves him and cares for him passionately, who would, when the chips are down, always put him first, who will put up with a fair degree of discomfort, distress, sheer exhaustion for his sake, if necessary. But at the same time I want him to understand that I have a life of my own, which I value as a part of myself that is not given over to him. Work is a fulfilment he cannot bring me; the friendships I have are not his domain and they own a part of me which is not his. It has always seemed important that he should understand that I too have needed separation from him. There have been times when his wish for a MacDonald's, his request to be chauffered here and there, to be amused because he is bored, have had to be put aside because I was preoccupied with *my* thing.

I have felt it vital that he know I consider myself too good for his or any chap's bovver boots to trample over me. And there have been times, sharing the home with Zek, his younger brother Cato and their father, when I have felt in danger of disappearing under the weight of their macho postering, their determination to be tough and hard. I may know that underneath they are

131

vulnerable, sensitive, uncertain just as I am, but their way of dealing with it is to prove the opposite.

I have, then, determinedly stood up for my rights, for recognition of my value as a woman doing things a womanly way and I have talked it out with Zek so that now, as a gangling 17-year-old, he will quite often jump to my defence if the testosterone factor is getting out of control in our home. I have felt it vital Zek and Cato understand that men and women are not the same, that the essential gender blend is very different, but that difference does not imply either superiority or inferiority. Remembering the words of Sigmund Freud: 'Above all a man looks for the memory picture of his mother as it has dominated him since the beginning of his childhood'. It seemed these things should be part of that memory. And it has always seemed that tough love, to coin the American term, was the name of the game.

Battling all this out from toddler to teenhood with two boys, has involved no small amount of opposition to my lads' essential maleness. Like the time one announced that he would simply beat up anyone who didn't do as he wanted in his garden; like the occasion six-year-old Zek snuggled deep into our bed and commanded: 'Go downstairs, make a cup of tea and do it quick!' Or like the time Cato, aged four, told me: 'Men are better than women. They can do anything. Women only have babies.' And equally I've felt it necessary the times their maleness has been so clearly detrimental to themselves. The most vivid example is when Cato, aged 13, went to the cinema with friends and was assaulted outside by a gang of some fifteen large kids simply because he went to a different school to them. They kicked him, put a plastic bag over his head and when that was off the ringleader punched him on the jaw. Not surprisingly Cato was upset, frightened, humiliated. He was tearful and I wanted to wrap him in my arms, let him howl a bit and talk about his feelings. But no, he felt he must seem tough in the face of all this and fought back the tears while talking of what he would do if he saw the gang again. What a price being seen to be an invulnerable male extracts from our sons.

The issues which come up when our boys voice their knee-jerk views on women seem important as subjects for discussion. I believe loving them means understanding why they see things the way they do, where their information on male-female differences is coming from. I have doggedly tried to involve them in discussion asking for example why, if women can only have babies, they occupy some very important jobs. 'Heavy...' my partner would sigh, but thinking of the future women in these youngsters lives, my duty as a mother committed to not adding to the population of male chauvinist pigs, has loomed large.

But I hit a real conflict over the meaning of what loving is all about when it came to combining my career with Zek. When he was born, the drive by women to prove they could do the same jobs as men, to reach all the best boardrooms, had begun, and for many it entailed playing the male role of virtually living at work to prove their dedication. I had a full-time job on a newspaper at the time and returned when Zek was four months old. Suddenly our life was perpetual motion and perpetual exhaustion; delivering and collecting from the child minder, frantic shopping, the launderette and housework. My overwhelming wish by the time I got home each evening was for one of us to get the baby to bed as quickly as possible so that we could put our feet up.

Then it hit me – this small person had become the most dispensable thing in life. Evening after evening I was wishing my child, whom I hadn't seen all day, out of the way. Great. As he grew up would his view of women be that they were high achievers with no time for love, companionship or relaxation? Would women personify the very things we have protested about in men so loudly?

I left my full-time job and went freelance, and although my bank balance developed anorexia, I had several extra hours in the day in which I could play with my son, get cross with him and make it up, cuddle him, let him know what it was to have a woman who loved him around the place. And it still seems to me that any love relationship needs time, energy and involvement to make it strong.

I have shared views with other mothers believing, as we are all cutting our way through unknown territory, that sharing experiences is valuable. One who has life organised so that she leaves work on time and can be with her children from the minute she gets back says: 'To me it's all important that I have time to work out the things I care about with my children, and with the boy there are very real bits of male culture I dislike. It's not just a question of saying: "I don't want you to have guns – they're nasty". It's having time to sit down and discuss why and how guns are used, why they appeal to boys more than girls. We owe it to our sons to help them break with the patterns of behaviour they grow up with, because they don't make women unhappy. I think all that 'I don't feel nuffin' maleness makes them unhappy too.'

And another, Ruth Cadby, a single parent with a son speaking when he was 12, explained: 'I am very demanding of Sam. I expect him to make allowances for what I want and need to do with my time, I make a good deal of

134

the fact that I am as good a wage earner as a man would be, but I also devote a lot of energy to getting him to talk about his feelings, to oppose the very aggresive, tough-guy stuff he picks up at school, and I know he is a sensitive, caring boy, a boy who knows how to open up his feelings. There are things I feel less comfortable about as he reaches adolescence, but I think it has been important to consider what I was doing with Sam, what cause and effect there would be in his life.'

But there are issues other than the politics of women's liberation. A boy's view of female sexuality is inevitably drawn from what he experiences at home. Freud was 'dazzled' by the glimpse he got of his mother 'nudam' and while I doubt that Zek and Cato are dazzled by the sight of me, hopping blearily from bed to bathroom naked of a morning, I hope it will help them to feel at ease in a daily, domestic sort of way with women's bodies. And I am glad that they walk into our bedroom without knocking, to find us closely entwined, or that they clamber unself-consciously into the family bed.

On the other hand, when I have pushed the frontiers and become the coquette with my boys, flirting lightly, bringing a frisson to the relationship, it has made them uneasy and at times outraged and angry. Although as Zek has grown towards late teens that has shifted and now, from a height of 6'3" and with the *savoir faire* gained in the past couple of years, he is quite flirtatious with me. But I remember vividly when some years ago I asked him what he liked in our relationship and he replied: 'I like it that you talk to me and listen to me, but I hate it when you get silly and don't act like a proper mother'. These days, however, I am aware that he is pleased when I wear quite raunchy clothes and when one of the male staff at his school says something complimentary suggesting I am a sexual being.

Reflecting on time with two growing males I see that quite a chunk of it was constructing strategies and worrying about whether I was succeeding in casting two fully re-constructed men to the world. But there was also time when I just let myself enjoy being mother to two kids I adore because of who they are, their gender mix, not in spite of a good world (while thinking some of the bad side products need erasing), I watch with amusement the boldness and enthusiasm my younger son takes in his male existence, and I feel sure that loving and enjoying them for what they are is also important in helping them to grow into men who will feel good about themselves and be able to be good to others.

But of course it is not all about bringing up a right-on chap. Returning to the essential point that a mother is the first love in a son's life and the mother's love for a son is very particular, passionate and poignant, how does this feeling evolve? I remember when Zek was just five and very taken by the slightly older daughter of my best friend. He was invited to her party. As she prepared to troop upstairs with a couple of girls he tried to join them. She turned and with a look of utter disdain said to him: 'Only my friends are allowed upstairs.' I watched my son's face drain; I could see the tears in his eyes, the frantic biting of the lip as he turned dejectedly away. And oh the fury I felt with this young madam who had rejected my precious boy.

But as that childlike vulnerability which used to assure me of unrivalled supremacy as the woman in my first son's life made way for a surface sophistication, and an often disdainful adolescence where I felt myself excluded from his thoughts and actions more and more, my feelings changed. One summer I got the first glimpse of the loss to come. On a river beach in France, he met an exquisitely pretty French girl, a couple of years younger. As she sat in an effortless lotus position, smiling at us, clearly wishing to be approached, he shuffled, shy and ungainly, towards her and perched on a rock near enough to speak to her, but far enough not to appear especially interested, and in the most painfully fractured, schoolboy French, he attempted to converse. I watched, amused, indulgent at the gauche antics of my son and, seeing myself as the experienced mediator, I joined in asking the girl questions. It was profound miscalcultion. Zek turned on me, red in the face with anger, an antipathy which was quite shocking. He then got up and left.

Another lesson was the occasion of a few years later when, attempting to find out what kind of sexual attitudes and knowledge my boys had, I tried a little *insouciant* questioning. Suddenly my 13-year-old, eyes blazing turned on me: 'Of course we don't want to tell you about our sexual urges!'

I had come to realise that the love and passion which my sons had directed at me all their growing years would, in due course, be redirected towards some other woman. They might, and hopefully will, continue to love me in a benign way, allotting me the quota of love appropriate to a Mum from whom they are growing away, but each will want and choose to be with another woman. The concern then will be not how they will take the experience of loving me on to future relationships, but how I, as a mother, will cope with losing that early love.

But while grappling with worries about future girl-friends and daughter-in-laws, I realise that I must help them to make that transition. The brief attempt made by Zek on the river beach has not, in front of me, been repeated, but there are certainly references nowadays to girls he likes and a lot of chat and laughter when he's cooped up in his room with mates. So what is my role now? To continue encouraging the puppy dog embraces he gives me, at the same time allowing his love to be transferred to another woman when the time comes...

What a lot of thought goes into it all and yet for them it is just growing up, a process which happens as it happens, unselfconsciously; they cannot be aware of the turmoil at times when I feel I should do or have done things, or the intense miraculous joy of knowing that I can share at least some of my life with these two unfathomable males. Probably as they swagger off into their own lives they'll dismiss all these maternal feelings as Noel Coward did. 'Mother love is a highly respected and much publicised emotion, and when exacerbated by gin and bourbon, it can become extremely formidable.'

Never try and make a woman
HAPPY - she'll only
resent it ..

'He doesn't woo me like that any more.'

Erin Pizzey founder of the Womens Refuge movement her
novels include *Swimming with Dolphins* and
*For The Love of A Stranger*.

•

Whenever I have fallen in love it's been under the
influence of gin. The sight of a large crystal glass
filled to the brim with that clear white liquid topped with
the prickly bubbled tonic water is mesmerizing. Almost as
mesmerizing as the beloved's eyes.

The trouble with me is that I'm an incurable romantic.
All my loves have been chosen for their propensity for
bringing flowers and bottles of wine. It gets me into a
terrible amount of trouble but I have a wonderful lawyer
– well three actually – that's how many lawyers it takes to
keep me out of trouble.

I was subjected to an attempted rape a while back. As I
struggled with my assailant (and he was strong at six foot
something) I wondered what chance women had if this
was how he behaved when he simply invited me to lunch?
'I only wanted to exchange the *The Times Literary Supple-
ment* for your *Economist*', I explained. The absurdly
annoying thing about all this rolling about is that my
friends all howl with laughter when I complain. 'It's no
laughing matter say I.' The other day I gave my usual
speech to a photographer. 'Fanta my alsatian is terribly
violent and aggressive so be careful. If she thinks you are
upsetting me she will savage you.' I looked down to find

141

Fanta on her back with her legs in the air waiting for the photographer to tickle her tummy.

The bad Baron was just as bad. I ended up brandishing a very large kitchen knife at his chest and saying, 'now love if you don't stop talking about sex at my dinner table you will spend the night in the garden.' I spent the night with my door locked guarded by four large dogs.

Of course there are the married men. They just have to have sex said one moody gentleman. Actually he was no gentleman. Another offered to visit me in Italy. I am writing to him to tell him why not. Oh why are all the best men married? These days the single men on the loose you wouldn't wish on your worst enemy. You see I'm always on the side of the wife. I don't care if she's a rotten two bit gold plated whore. She's a woman and therefore my sister.

My favourite lover and my only lover was South African. He looked like Jesus and he was a carpenter. We had a wonderful time together and did good things for each other, but all good things come to an end. We waved each other goodbye and I shall always remember him with love and affection.

As I sit in my forest surrounded by the natural beauty of Tuscany, I dream of my home in the Cayman Islands. The nightingales sing me to sleep and I wake up with the farm animals yelling good morning. Who ever said the countryside was quiet?

I've forsworn love for a while and by the way I drink Brandy and Soda. Until the next time that is.

Paddy Ashdown MP for Yeovil, former commando in the Marines, is now leader of the Liberal Democrats.

●

I was only 18½ when I met my wife Jane. At that time I was in the Marines and the rule was you could only get married after the age of 25. I actually quite disgracefully got married 10 days before my 21st birthday in 'military sin'. We had to ask the permission of the Lords of the Admiralty in order to do so and even then it remained difficult. We weren't allowed quarters or marriage allowances and as my job required me to go abroad a lot, Jane had to make her way to see me by hitching lifts on RAF aircraft around the world.

Colin Dunne, writer and journalist contributes to a variety of glossy magazines and is author of several thrillers.

•

When I got into school the morning after my evening at Dickie Bones' flat, all the other boys gathered round. They were desperate to know. What had happened? What was his wife like? What had he said? 'Nothing much, bit boring,' I said, and, disappointed, they turned away. I was lying, of course. He'd changed my life.

I'd had a special claim on Dickie Bones ever since that first morning of term, when we'd finished our ritualistic 'Lord Receive Us With Thy Blessing', and I'd been the first to see him as he came loping up the long slope of the school drive. 'Hello, a native bearer,' he said, with a matey grin. 'I'm Richardson-Jones. Can you guide me to the art-room?' Even by the standards of art teachers, he was quite something: brown curls bubbling over ears and collar, cord trousers only half-an-inch off drainpipes, gaudy jacket and knitted tie, he wasn't like any teacher I'd seen before.

Our grammar school, in a cold northern market town, was as formal as a medieval church. The masters (teachers was far too flippant a word) were the high priests, in their regalia of sports jackets and university ties, flannels and softly-gleaming brogues. We were the peasants, who got our Latin prep in on time, played rugby until our thighs were blue from blizzards, and

145

whose most daring dissent was a cap tilted one degree off the obligatory horizontal. Masters did not smile at boys, matily or otherwise, they didn't say hello to them, and they certainly didn't talk in this easy, jokey way.

I sped back with the news. Sure enough, at the first art lesson, he didn't let me down. 'Right,' he said, 'let's get that ceiling down a bit. Black, d'you reckon, Dunne? What about the walls? Purple to bring that one in, yellow for the facing wall ...' By the time we'd finished, the room looked like a fairground, and the whole school was buzzing with rumour that a wild man was among us.

Gentle, humorous, informal, he never even tried to teach: instead, he talked. He talked about the power of colour and shape, the emotion that fired a work of art, the frenzied lives of great artists, what they were trying to say when they picked up a brush, and we blossomed in the warmth of his passion like flowers in the sun. Before the week was out he was Dickie Bones. His reputation grew, but we could never separate rumour from reality. Was it true that the headmaster, a man who prided himself on beating a whole form alphabetically and still making the last boy cry (Woods and Windles had a hard time at my school), loathed him because he declined to attend school rugby games? Had he really once said he didn't believe in exams? Did he really have a wife like the women we had only seen on the Plaza screen? Could it be possible that he played in a jazz-band and drank in pubs?

What was even more extraordinary was the way he shattered the conventional understanding between boys and masters.

Elsewhere, troublemakers were punished by being made to stay longer in the classroom, in detention. Since he considered that the greatest punishment was to be excluded from his lessons, he tossed them out. For boys whose sole ambition was to escape from a classroom, at first this seemed splendid. Then, slowly, even the most stupid of them began to sense the shame of exile. They were missing out on something.

Every spare moment I had was spent in the art room, listening to Dickie Bones. I longed, I think, not so much for the skill of painting, which in my case was vestigial, but for whatever mystery it was that he seemed to represent: which was a glimpse of a world that was full of excitement, drama, and an outrageous glamour. Although I didn't know it then, he was a dissident, belonging to that distinguished elite who, from the Bohemians to today's Alternatives, see no merit in conforming.

'If you want to know how an artist sees the world, Dunne,' he said, one day, 'get down to the library and ask for The Horse's Mouth.' I read it to the end in one go, and then started at the beginning again. The novel by Joyce Cary, a brilliant and now sadly forgotten writer, showed me a life that knew no rules. It was also rude. When asked what he thought of modern art, the painter hero – if I remember correctly – said: 'It's rather like farting Annie Laurie through a keyhole – it's clever, but does it get you anywhere?'

The other boys were incredulous: a master had recommended a book which contained, in clear and undeniable print, the word *farting*. These days it's probably on the school curriculum as a sport, but then it was dangerous stuff.

'Music, art, it's all the same, Dunne,' said Dickie Bones, packing me off to the library again, this time in search of 'Mister Jelly Roll,' by Alan Lomax, a book about Jelly Roll Morton, the New Orleans jazzman who played in a brothel. Our first-hand knowledge of brothels in the Yorkshire Dales was, in those days, limited, but I had a feeling that it beat the hell out of youth-club table-tennis. In the local record shop, gathering dust on a shelf, I found my first 78. Across the three thousand miles and the forty years that separated us, his creole voice, anguished with rapture, cried: 'Ah, hellow central, give me Doctor Jazz', and I was lost. Forever.

After that, under Dickie Bones' direction, came Steinbeck and Hemingway and Faulkner, Greene and Waugh, and when I wasn't painting, I was listening, and when I wasn't listening, I was reading.

I was basking in reflected glory. After all, I had a special claim on him. I had seen him first. I was his native bearer. I was also, for the first time, top in art. Latin, French, English Lit... all of them fell by the wayside.

'Dunne,' wrote the headmaster in my report, 'appears to have taken up art at the expense of all his other studies, a characteristically perverse decision.' He predicted 'O' level failure in everything except art, a forecast which incited my father to hurl my report book across the room.

I didn't care. I was a rebel. I was Van Gogh Jelly Roll Dunne and I marched to a different drum.

Then, to my astonishment, the invitation to his house. Because my pocket money, even inflated with paper-round wages, only allowed for four new records a year, my collection was a little slow in growing. 'Come round and listen to some records, Dunne,' he said. To his house? Yes. Me? Yes. To a master's? It was all too heady.

When I got there, I had my tie undone and my socks wrinkled to show that I too belonged to the rule-breakers, farters and brothel-clients and famous writers who lived for their art and were prepared to risk wearing a shirt without a name tag. As I went in, I saw, hanging on the wall, a trombone. Did he really play in a band? Oh, he said, he used to, but he didn't have much time these days.

I was inside the house of a genuine jazzman.

'Do you drink beer?' he asked. At 15, I had once had a shandy on holiday. 'Quite a bit, actually,' I said, striving to give the impression that I poured the stuff over my cornflakes.

'Bring Colin a beer,' he called through to the kitchen as he put on a record of 'SOL Blues' by Louis Armstrong. 'Know what SOL stands for?' he asked. 'Shit Outa Luck.'

I was inside the house of a genuine jazzman who called me by first name and had just said shit.

All the time I was trying to keep my eyes off a huge portrait over the mantelpiece of a beautiful woman who was, it appeared to me, with little expertise in this area, to be naked. Dickie Bones was the first to mention it. He hadn't got the set of the neck quite right, he said, although the set of the neck seemed one of its least interesting features. My experience of naked women was at the same level as my drinking.

I was inside the house of a genuine jazzman who called me by my first name, said shit and was talking about naked women.

At that moment, the door opened and in came a very beautiful woman indeed, bearing my beer (in, I now realise, something the size of a sherry-glass), and she smiled at me and said hello. I stammered, I stuttered, I wriggled, and my face glowed, a beacon of embarrassment. It was his wife. It was also the woman in the picture. Try as I could, as she handed me my beer, I could not see this pleasant woman modestly clad in shirt and skirt, but only the naked body on the wall.

I was inside the house of a genuine jazzman who called me by my first name, said shit, and I was drinking beer handed to me for all intents and purpose by a naked woman.

He talked of books and writers and music and painting, although, for once, rendered mute by ecstasy, I took little of it in. In the Yorkshire Dales in those days, a nude, a beer, and Louis Armstrong was every bit as potent as sex, drugs and rock 'n' rock to a later generation. A little sadly, the next day I realised that if I told the truth at school, no-one would believe me. 'Nothing much, a bit boring,' I said, and they drifted away.

There was another reason too that had nothing to do with credibility: it was all far too precious to share.

When the exam results came in, I passed everything, except art. ' I told you exams are a waste of time,' said Dickie Bones. We sang 'Lord Dismiss Us With Thy Blessing,' and left. When we came back the next term, Dickie Bones had gone too. The headmaster smiled when he made the announcement. Desolate as I felt, I still knew he had changed me. Doors had been opened which now could never be closed.

Dickie Bones taught me about love. Love of painting, love of music, love of books and, yes, I suppose, love of beer and naked ladies and breaking rules. His lesson wasn't about art at all: it was about the love of life. Every time I hear that voice wail: 'Ah, hellow Central, give me Doctor Jazz..' I think about him.

Thanks Dickie Bones

Jeannette Kupfermann journalist, TV critic for *The Daily Mail*
and writer, her books include *When the Crying's Done* from
which her contribution to this book was extracted.

•

Perhaps the most painful and difficult part of writing
for this book has been remembering and describing
Jacques' cruel illness itself. It was something I blocked out
for a long time, until a newspaper headline proclaiming
that Rex Harrison had died of cancer of the pancreas
jolted me into remembering and looking back at the
detailed journal I kept at the time. I go back and relive the
grief of that winter of 1987.

Jacques reclines in the 'relaxing' garden chair – his
swollen legs on Mina's needlework stool – pillows in
his back. His face is pale, shrunken, hollow-eyed,
with a look of desperation – his lips colourless: with
his wispy white hair he looks so heart-breakingly
frail, the little orphaned boy, and my heart is heavy
with anguish for him.

I feel every pain – every twinge in his achingly
sore diaphragm. The illness has raged now for three
or so months – first the diarrhoea – then the terrible
pain – then the swellings on his ankles, legs and
lumps on his shoulders, arms and hands. His whole
body is like one open wound – and I weep. I weep
for this man I love above everything and everyone

151

else: who has been my mother, father, friend, lover, comforter and mentor – my constant companion and ally – my husband of twenty-three years.

I pray silently for him – and all the time I fear the emptiness, the nothingness to come. I try not to grieve in advance. I sit with him at the hospital as he waits for his CT scan – and see him emerge shocked and traumatized. I watch the ghost-like patients in their dressing gowns: the husbands and comforting wives, daughters and mothers – and again, I weep for all of them...

That night he goes into shock: he is deeply depressed and does not want to stay in the house. We walk for an hour or so in the chill damp night air, my arm around his shrunken body. I feel closer than I have ever felt to him. I pick him a white rose from the garden on the hill and I have a vision of a white lily with a light shining on it. Tomorrow he will get the results. Jacques says he feels a sudden fear that he will not last the night. I give him whisky and water, and read him Psalm 112. He sleeps in his special chair by the side of my bed – and wakes, as usual, several times in the night.

We survive the night together. Another day dawns – and again. I start the breakfast – shop for calves' liver, make soup and wait. I think of our walks in Cliveden, the Japanese water garden he loves so... and I love him too – this poor frail, pain-ridden man, clutching at my hand beside me in the bed, propped up on pillows, the man who has been by my side for all these years – my *everything*. I want to take his pain into me. I pray, I read Psalms – I prepare the special vegetable and fruit juices he has been prescribed as part of the anti-cancer diet – do the lengthy washing out of the juice extractor machine – worry about him as he takes shaky walks on the terrace, listen for him as he spends long sessions in the bathroom with his radio. I watch his grey face over breakfast – anxiously listen to his breathing at night – listen to him heaving and writhing in pain – my man – the being I love most in the world who has given such love, beauty and devotion so silently, so undemandingly all these years, and my anguish knows no bounds. I want to tear out my hair – weep and wail – and yet I restrain myself – keep calm – keep coping – keep reassuring – present a face of optimism – go through the visualization exercises with him – relax him – stroke his hand, face and white hair – and devise a battle song to defeat this wicked disease.

'In the spring,' he sings, 'I will be better…'

Victor Olliver, journalist and writer contributes to magazines
and newspapers, he is currently writing his first novel.

•

I picked up the phone and heard the familiar croak. 'Hi
Ingrid.' I said. 'What's wrong today?'

'Darling,' she rasped, 'I've been poisoned. The bastard
put aluminium in the water tank and now I've got
Alzheimer's. I can't even remember why I called you.
Ugh.'

The 'bastard' was her ex-husband. After their acri-
monious divorce a court had recently allowed him to re-
enter the family home (which they still co-owned) and
occupy the downstairs. At once he had moved back in
with his 22 year old daughter from his first marriage.
Meanwhile, upstairs, Ingrid and her 17 year old daughter
(by the 'bastard') screamed at them both all day through
the floorboards.

Had he put the aluminium in the water tank? Who
knows. She was one of a small band of close friends whose
lives were endless melodramas, with me as sensitive
spectator. The more outlandish the life the bigger was my
heart. I might be exasperated at times by what I heard but
it seemed to me that the package of other people's affection tended to come with listening to them.

'The bastard has two other daughters by some other
cow, I've just read the first wife cow's affidavit,' Ingrid
sighed as she gently rolled her head, eyes shut, on the

pillow; a Jane Asher lookalike *a la* Breugel. I was now standing over her as she lay in her bed. 'But the clairvoyants say he's finished,' she said, her eyes now wide open. 'One day he'll just disappear.'

All around us were signs of irretrievable breakdown. The ceiling plaster cracked and flaked by the 'bastard's' vigorous storage activities in the loft – one could almost see the rafters. The suitcases on the landing. And the stethoscope draped over the staircase balustrade – so useful for late night espionage on downstairs, with the carpets turned back.

On the other side of the sick-bed stood Chrissie, co-ministering to Ingrid whose memory seemed unimpaired on the bastard's psychosis. Chrissie and I had once been in love, brought together again by another crisis in the life of a mutual friend. I hadn't seen her for some time. She still looked age 12 (though in her forties) but she had done something to her hair, what could it be? Did platinum blonde really suit an olive complexion? Oh well...

'You're not poisoned Ingrid,' diagnosed Chrissie, 'It's just your anger against the bastard...'

'Chrissie!' shouted Ingrid, lifting her head. 'Don't give me that crap. I've been POISONED – there's nothing, what's the word – I'm so Alzheimer-ish – I can't speak – there's nothing *psychological* about this...'

Chrissie and I had met at a psychics and mystics fair in Kensington three years earlier. A friend had recommended this tarot reader called Chrissie.

'I can't give you a reading,' had been her first words to me, 'because I feel too close to you.' It was an alarming but original chat-up line, and effective. I knew there and then what was foretold. I was about to fall for yet another gorgeous loony whose life would overwhelm me, exasperate me...

Back at Ingrid's Chrissie perched on the bed. 'Ingrid,' she said, 'It's all to do with your past life – no, listen, for a moment – in a previous life the bastard harmed you and now fate has brought you together again for karmic reasons. It's cause and effect – you have to beat him this time. Once you were his...'

'I know, his gay lover. Thank you Chrissie, that's helpful to know. You say it every time. When I had M.E. you said I had been a nun in a previous life and I was still trying to run from life. I'm sorry Chrissie but my problems are pure and simple organic. I respect your New Age beliefs but this is a straightforward case of poisoning. I can't eat carrots, cabbage, potatoes or anything grown in the earth because of the aluminium.' She smacked her lips – 'I can taste the metal. I might as well kill myself. Do you realise I have to microwave the water? You have no idea!'

'How do you know he poisoned you?'

Ingrid held Chrissie's gaze: 'I *know*.'

Christmas-time with Chrissie. We foraged for small fallen branches in the local forest to make up what she called a 'natural Christmas tree'. We scented ourselves in the bath with Bach flower oils to please the spirits. We detected a ley-line running through her kitchen. All the while I kept asking myself? Am I mad? Insincere?

One day we had booked into an inn in Arundel. Instantly Chrissie had decreed that the sheets would have to be rewashed in Ecover because she was allergic to the perfume in ordinary washing powders. 'The bananas must go – they're preserved in gas on the ships. And the telly. It has to face the wall. The electrons. I won't be able to sleep.' Oh God.

Yes, I'd wanted to say something – something like, 'For God's sake Chrissie, won't you give it a rest' – the sort of something that I was tempted to say now in Ingrid's bedroom, to both Ingrid and Chrissie. But what would I lose by saying it? I didn't want to test a friendship, any kind of relationship. I never did. Occasional exasperation seemed a small price to pay for... for what? An odd kind of intimacy.

The relationship with Chrissie had ended anyway when she announced, 'We're not soul mates, I was wrong.' Shortly afterwards I had another Chrissie-type: a driven my-world-is-your-world New Ager. And me, all quiet ferment.

Chrissie and I left Ingrid to her poisoning and walked down to the beach. 'It's good seeing you again,' she said. 'Ingrid is so sick, so angry. The hurt child in her – she's never recognised it, she's never faced it.'

'The child?'

'You're still so Gemini aren't you? I remember your horoscope: Sun in Gemini, ascendent in Gemini, moon in Pisces – you're six sided, no balance –'

I wanted to say 'Do shut up.'

'It makes you very mental, too detached...'

But I couldn't.

Richard E. Grant, stage, film and TV actor who has starred in
*The Player*, *Age of Innocence*, *Withnail and I*, *The Importance of
Being Earnest* and *Dracula*.

•

'YOUR WIFE IS ON HER WAY TO HOSPITAL BY
AMBULANCE' – 9am, last day of filming at
Shepperton and a ghastly sense of *deja-vu*; we lost our
baby daughter three years before. Born at 7 months, she
lived for half an hour. Burying our baby was the saddest
of sorrows.

Again we are at 7 months and nausea capsizes my heart
and head. Rush to Queen Charlotte's Hospital and the
'waters' have mercifully not broken. But blood spotting.
Panic, terror, tears. All night vigil and Mr Malvern offers
guarded reassurance; 'If your wife does not go into
premature labour, there is a chance. A CHANCE. However, she will have to remain here for the rest of her
pregnancy and move as little as possible.'

The outside world recedes instantly and the inside of
the ward is simultaneously protecting and imprisoning.
Three months bed-bound for Joan. I am contracted to do
another film and get to the hospital at 6am and leave at
8am and return at 7pm till 11pm. They waive the visiting
hour restrictions and life has a precarious new routine.
This baby means everything. We know she is a girl. We
know her name. We see her kick. We tell her to stay
inside. Safe.

WAITING. Interrupted by emergency scares and shuffling trolley up to the labour ward. Not yet. Not now. Hands held together tight. Eyes super-glued. All saying. And love so overwhelming, we could bust. As one.

A diet of NEIGHBOURS and GOING FOR GOLD with Mr Kelly, Hello! and Marks and Sparks is relief from the hospital nosh. Any diversion. However banal. PRISONER CELL BLOCK H. Laughing. Holding. Hoping.

Christmas day and they are both still 'inside'. Kindness and compassion from nurses that we will never forget.

'We cannot risk full term and will perform a caesarian section at 36 weeks.' Decision taken and the 4th of January dated. Four minutes to 1pm and a 4 pound bird-sized baby is briefly 'exhibited' through a glass panel, wrapped tight. Mother still anaesthetised. And water has jetted involuntarily from my eyes like water pistols and the overwhelming relief has tied my tongue.

One kind of waiting is over and now I sit beside an unconscious mother-wife and sleeping baby daughter and the relief and silence and profound love is all engulfing.

Suzanne Askham, writer and journalist contributes to
newspapers and magazines and is the author of *Company
Magazine's Top 100 Jobs* and *and Adventure Unlimited*.

•

I think the world is divided between those who believe
in dangerous living, and those who prefer to stay in
bed with a cup of cocoa. I am the cocoa sort: when I feel
the fear I run away from it and hide under the duvet.

Until, that is, I fell for a man who believes you're not
really alive unless you could be dead the next minute. At
first, I thought I could control his morbid urges by sitting
him in front of the television when the action program-
mes were on – lurid series like 999, and documentaries
about obviously crazed explorers walking barefoot to the
Pole, that sort of thing.

But he simply treated each programme as the source of
another idiotic idea, to be put into action at the first
available opportunity. So I became an action fraud. We
trekked for hundreds of miles together, climbed dangerous mountain ridges. And I have to admit that I loved
the places we reached.

One sport I'd never taken to, though, was water. The
smell of chlorine, the splashy din of an indoor swimming
pool – it still makes me shiver with awful memories of
school swimathons. Paddling from a hot beach was fine,
but you'd never catch *me* out of my depth.

And then, he decided to join a scuba-diving club. 'It'll

be fantastic,' he raved. My heart sank; but I knew the rest of me would follow soon.

I couldn't see anything fantastic about this frogman business at all. These people put 20 pounds of lead around their waists, a great heavy cylinder on their backs, stick an air hose in their mouth and then roll backwards off a boat into cold, opaque British waters. They're crazy.

But I knew I had to learn how to do this terrible thing, just so I could be there to save him if anything went wrong.

First, over long, slow weeks, I learnt to swim proper lengths, without – as had been my sneaky habit in the past – turning round before I reached the deep end.

After that, I had to learn how to do it all underwater. I joined his club, and went through the basics, including unnerving and seemingly endless safety measures, in a deep London pool. Then we went to sea.

Now we fin along together, in and out of sunken shipwrecks, along gullies lined with waving kelp and pale sponges, beside underwater cliffs glowing purple with fairy anemones. There's one place we go, near Lindisfarne, where the seals come up from behind and nudge us playfully before speeding away, very likely laughing as they fade into the distance and then return for more.

In the water we're weightless; we fly like Superman simply by pointing our heads the way – up, down, sideways or diagonally – we want to go. It's just like dreaming, and it's stunning.

Of course, you can't talk underwater. But in the air bubbles that float up above me, you must just be able to read the words: 'I can't believe how much I love this thing I did for love!'

It makes me wonder about other things that seem alarming. I do now believe it's always worth looking beyond the fear barrier. There could just be something in this dangerous living after all.

**Bruce Forsyth acclaimed comedian, singer and TV star, hosts his own TV show as well as the enduring *Generation Game*.**

●

When I first started going out with my wife Winnie some 12 years ago, I'd always order broccoli whenever we went out for a meal because I knew she loved it. What she didn't know was that I didn't. I like almost every other vegetable but I can't stand broccoli.

Many years later we were sitting in front of the TV when George Bush came on and declared that he hated broccoli, and I blurted out 'So do I!'

Winnie looked at me and said, 'What do you mean? You love broccoli.'

So I had to tell her the truth. I said, 'I've eaten it all these years because I love you.'

Now I don't have to pretend any more.

Trudi Pacter, journalist and writer, her best selling novels
include *Kiss and Tell*, *Screen Kisses*, *Living Doll*. Her latest novel
is *Yellow Bird*.

•

I didn't mean to fall in love. It wasn't what I was being
paid for. My brief was to interview a certain movie star
about his divorce, then return to my newspaper with the
goods.

Which is what I did. Only somewhere along the way I
got led astray. It happened when he started talking about
his diet. There I was sitting in a glass and chrome interior
decorated penthouse, when this glossy celebrity comes on
like a human being.

It turned out he had this terrible problem with his
weight. He'd tried all the regimes, and just like the rest of
us he put back the pounds every time he went out and had
a decent meal.

Then he asked me if I was interested in having dinner
with him.

Before I could make an excuse and leave, he went on to
explain that this wasn't any old dinner. It was an event put
on to celebrate his birthday.

All his friends had been invited to a private room in an
exclusive restaurant and his big problem was he didn't
have a date.

I must have looked sceptical for he fell over backwards
describing how difficult it was for a man like him to find a

girl who genuinely liked him. Most of the women he knew wanted to use him for his fame and his money. Then he said he thought I was different.

I fell for it of course. And while I was about it, I fell for him. Which is why I took out the money I had put aside to pay the telephone bill and invested it in a dazzling dress for my movie star's birthday party.

I had been summoned to his apartment at seven o'clock. And when I turned up he answered the door himself. The first thing I noticed was that he was wearing jeans. I was all dolled up in floor length black velvet, and my date was in denims.

Naturally I asked if I had got there too early. Perhaps he wasn't quite ready? He shook his head, ushered me through to the main room. And I realised my mistake. For everyone was in casuals. It was that sort of evening. Only nobody had thought to tell me.

My humiliation was complete when my glamorous escort took me to one side and told me he had an idea. Why didn't one of his friends give me a lift home on the way to the restaurant so I could change.

The friend who took me home was Roman Polanski. And it was clear the whole situation amused the hell out of him.

I didn't think it was funny at all. When I finally turned up at the birthday party in slacks and a sweater, I knew the romance wasn't going to get off the ground. I had made the grand gesture, spent a lot of money I didn't have because I believed myself to be in love. And I got the whole thing thrown back in my face.

After that I interviewed a lot of actors. Faithfully writing down everything they said in my reporter's notebook. Only I had the good sense never to believe a word any of them told me again.

166

Mike Molloy, writer journalist and former editor of *The Daily Mirror* and Editor in Chief of *MGN*. His books include *Century*, *Sweet Sixteen*, *Cats Paw* and *Home Before Dark*.

●

1956 started badly for me: on January 5, Prince Rainier III of Monaco announced his engagement to Grace Kelly: so there I was, two weeks after my fifteenth birthday, standing at a bus stop at Hanger Lane in the rain, with only the gusting wind to know the secrets of my troubled heart. Why couldn't she have waited? I asked myself over and over again – she'd waited for William Holden in The Bridges at Toko Ri.

My misery was made even more profound by the earliness of the hour. Our sadistic Headmaster had recently devised a new addition to his repertoire of punishments: morning detention. Those guilty of minor offences were ordered to attend school half an hour before the normal time and read passages of *Silas Marner* to each other. A device that was not intended to instil in us an appreciation of English Literature; but a hatred of lady novelists, a breed to which he was particularly opposed on some obscure moral grounds.

In my case this was an exceptionally unpleasant imposition, not that I had anything against George Eliot, but I did have an almost pathological hatred of getting up in the dark.

Eventually the bus arrived and I shuffled aboard. The

top deck smelt of stale tobacco as it always did; but at this earlier time of day there was a different array of school uniforms to the ones I was used to at my normal hour. These were like soldiers from a Napoleonic army: chocolate, sky blue, scarlet, Connacht green; and then I spotted a pair of blazers similar to my own, the dullest of navy blue.

They were worn by two classmates, Reid and Parsons who, like me, were reporting for an early morning dose of *Silas Marner*. I joined them near the front of the bus and took the empty seat ahead of them.

Because there were no adults on the top deck, Reid and Parsons were sharing a surreptitious cigarette. It was an act of reckless bravery on their part, considering the savage penalties imposed by our Headmaster for such a transgression. Not wearing one's cap was considered a crime grave enough to incur corporal punishment; smoking was a hanging offence.

They sought to disguise their dangerous pleasure by alternately ducking down, heads between their knees before taking turns to inhale from the Senior Service now held between Reed's nicotine stained fingers. Clouds of blue smoke billowed up between their lips, betraying their illicit pursuit just as surely as smoke signals from an Indian camp fire.

'Want a drag?' Reid offered, flashing the disgusting remains as I turned to face them.

'I'd rather eat cold chips from a leper's loincloth' I replied coldly, my mood was still bleak after the news issued by the Grimaldis and I was unready for the callow pleasures of these careless youths.

Reid shrugged and ducked down again – then I saw the girl who sat behind him.

I will not attempt to describe her; just make your own journey to the Uffizi Gallery in Florence; ask where Botticelli's Venus hangs; stand before the picture and image her wearing a gym slip and a jade coloured blazer.

Grace Kelly's ice maiden looks faded from my memory like a shovel of snow held over a bonfire – only to be instantly replaced by this new vision of loveliness.

Could hair really be the colour of flames dancing in an Autumn fire? I ask myself, as I sat gazing helplessly at her; my face muscles slack with wonder. She avoided my stare with a haughty indifference that made her seem even more desirable and turned to her companion with whom she talked in an animated fashion until they rose from their seats as the bus approached their stop on Ealing Common. Heart pounding, I wanted desperately to follow her slender form. Then I noticed the friend accompanying her, who looked down at me as they passed. There was something familiar about her more curvaceous figure; it was Valerie Rodmere, a girl who lived next door to my Aunt Bella in Wembley Park. A tentative link, I quickly decided, but one which I might be able to forge into a stronger chain.

The following Saturday morning I was exhausted after the passage of two turbulent nights. Each time I had attempted sleep in the past forty-eight hours the vision of the red-headed girl had filled my mind's eye with such force it had driven out any possibility of rest. Rising from my storm-tossed bed soon after sunrise, I set off for Wembley Park and the road where Aunt Bella resided.

In happier times I could have made her house my headquarters for the enterprise I'd set about; but the difficulty was Aunt Bella and I were not exactly on speaking terms. On Christmas Eve she caught me and her son, Geoffrey, attempting to determine wether it was possible to leave a footprint in the cold custard that was topping a large bowl of sherry trifle she had prepared. Not wishing to infect the pudding with any noxious matter that clung to the soles of our own footwear, Geoffrey had suggested we use a new pair of bedroom slippers Aunt Bella had purchased as a Christmas present for my Uncle Henry. Although Geoffrey had been the driving force behind the experiment, I had been deemed the instigator of the offence as I was three weeks older than he; and therefore judged the more mature partner in the crime.

If my aunt and uncle had heard the boasts of what cousin Geoffrey had done in Barham Park with the local girl of ill-repute, all thought of immaturity would have drained from their minds; and Geoffrey would have properly been considered by them as only fit for the company of elderly degenerates.

But as things stood, Aunt Bella would not welcome my presence at 'Four Winds', the preposterously named semi-detached house where she resided. Therefore, my plan was to walk slowly up and down her street, ducking down outside 'Four Winds' lest Aunt Bella should spot me whilst gazing from her window; and wait for Valerie Rodmere to appear. I was confident that Valerie would leave her house sometime during the day; it was only a matter of patience.

Actually she finally emerged on Sunday afternoon; clutching a pair of ice skating boots. It was all I could to catch up with her on legs that had become rubbery from trudging up and down the street where she lived.

'Hello, Valerie,' I said in what I hoped was a nonchalant voice as I drew level.

She actually seemed pleased to see me. 'Hello,' she answered. 'I haven't seen you in a long time.'

'What about the other morning?'

'I didn't think you noticed me,' she replied.

'Course I did,' I replied quickly. 'You were with that girl from your school… you know the one… what's her name?'

Valerie looked at me for a moment and then said: 'Anne Fenton.'

'That's her,' I replied clicking my finger. 'Anne Fenton – good friend of yours, is she?'

'The best one I have.'

I thought this was unusual – girls as beautiful as Anne Fenton normally had a best friend chosen for the homeliness of their looks; and Valerie was something of a stunner in her own way, if you happened to fancy freckles and a body like an Italian film star. My cousin Geoffrey certainly did – he had a collection of drawings he had composed entitled: What I'm Going To Do To The Girl Next Door.

'What's she like, Anne Fenton?' I continued, my voice breaking slightly when I uttered her name. 'Popular, is she – lots of boy friends?'

Valerie paused again. 'Actually she's very shy, it takes her ages to make new friends. She'll only go out with a boy if she's known him for a long time.'

By now we had reached the bus stop from where Valerie would journey to the ice rink at the Empire Pool.

'Do you both catch the same bus to school every morning?' I asked.

Valerie nodded. 'We meet here at eight o'clock.' Then she put out her hand to hail the approaching bus. As it also took me to Hanger Lane, I got on with her and we sat chatting about Anne Fenton until she got off at the Empire Pool.

For the rest of the way home I formulated a plan. If I caught a bus to Wembley Park at seven o'clock each morning, I should be able to effect a casual meeting with Valerie and Anne Fenton at their bus stop. Then I would be able to travel all the way to Ealing Common with them; and in the fullness of time, say three or four days, I should be able to ask Anne Fenton if we could meet alone. Feeling that I now shared a certain intimacy with Valerie Rodmere, I telephoned her later that evening to confess my feelings, confide my plan and seek her co-operation.

'Leave it to me,' she said firmly. 'I'll fix things for you.'

Valerie's offer of help made me light-headed with happiness, the only problem now was money; the extra travelling each day would cost me at least another ten shillings a week and taking Anne Fenton to the cinema each Saturday would cost at least another pound.

Thirty shillings every week; the sum was daunting. Getting it from my parents was out of the question. The only solution was some sort of work.

As if to prove Jung's theory of synchronocity, the following week I heard of a paper round that had fallen vacant some miles from my home. It seemed the gods smiled on my intentions. My application was successful and I made plans to begin immediately.

Such was the power of Anne Fenton's loveliness, I now had to rise from my bed at five a.m. each morning to cycle to where my paper round was located if I wished to complete my duties in time to catch the bus to Wembley Park so that I could casually bump into Valerie Rodmere and the object of my desire each day.

Anthony Trollope, the prolific Victorian novelist,

boasted that he rose each morning at five a.m. and by breakfast time had completed his day's work. What he didn't point out was that if you attempt to imitate such a regime in the particular circumstances I endured, you were likely to fall soundly asleep just as you were expected to give your most earnest attentions to the mysteries of the Renaissance.

Nonetheless, Anne Fenton was worth it, I told myself as I strolled towards the bus stop where Valerie Rodmere stood that first morning. My heart jumped when I saw the flame coloured hair of her companion; but as I approached, I saw Valerie hold up a warning hand. Heeding the signal, I lingered some distance away and did not attempt conversation. As I got on the bus, Valerie thrust a note into my hand.

It read: Anne is too shy to speak to you. She says she would prefer it if you wrote to her for a while, so she can get to know you gradually. The problem is, her parents are very strict. If they find any letters from a boy they will forbid her from seeing you. She suggests you write them to me, so if her parents should find one of them she will appear to be innocent.

I nodded my understanding at a suitable moment and gave Valerie the thumbs up sign as she was getting off the bus.

That night I began yet another new task in life: persuading Anne Fenton, by prose alone, that I was worthy of her affections. It was hard work. Love letters, I discovered, are best written in a mood of insincerity. Every genuine word seems shallow, false and wooden when you attempt to write from the heart. But finally, a few hours before I was due to ride off to start the paper round, I slipped the laboured pages into an envelope and slept briefly.

Extraordinary as it seems to me now, this pattern of behaviour lasted several weeks, although I did start writing the letters at a more convenient time – during lunch hours I seem to remember. I still had not managed to speak to Anne Fenton; but I was now seeing a great deal of Valerie; she had began to invite me to her home on Saturday to discuss the situation. It was a good time, she explained, because her mother and father were always working in their chemist shop in Edgware and we would not be disturbed.

The third Saturday I arrived at the usual time and Valerie was taking a bath.

'I wasn't expecting you so soon,' she said as she ushered me into her bedroom. The towel that she wore doing little to hide her voluptuous figure. My resolve weakened, probably by lack of sleep, Valerie's slipping towel and a question I had been asking myself more and more in recent weeks. The question was instantly answered. She did have freckles everywhere. Moments later we were grappling on the bed.

'Wait,' Valerie gasped and she darted from the room to return instantly with a packet of French letters which she explained were stock from her parent's chemist shop that the kept in the house.

Afterwards we lay gazing at the celing like they did in foreign films and I said: 'I suppose I'd better write to Anne and tell her it's all over between us.'

'There's writing paper on my desk,' Valerie answered. 'I'll see that she gets it.'

'At least I'll be able to give up the paper round,' I said wistfully.

'You need your sleep,' Valerie agreed.

I never did speak to Anne Fenton – that Easter she

moved to Rhodesia. Valerie gave me the news the day we broke up.

'Why are you doing this?' I asked, bewildered by her change of heart.

'All you want me for is sex,' she complained bitterly. 'You never write to me the way you used to do.'

I suppose some women are never satisfied.

You're greedy, hostile,
depressed, childish,
selfish, angry,
moody, mean,
jealous,
difficult
and
... IMPOSSIBLE!

She CARES!

Ivan Fallon, deputy editor of *The Sunday Times*, his books include *The Brothers; The Story of Saatchi and Saatchi* and *Billionaire: The Life And Times of Sir James Goldsmith*.

•

Perhaps the most durable and powerful love of my life has been brotherly love. I was born the fifth of six brothers, fifteen years separating the youngest, Padriac, from the eldest, Garry. We lived on the south coast of Ireland in a large rambling old house, within range of rivers, mountains and the sea, all of which we used to the full.

From the moment I could walk, I had to march behind the others as Garry, a self-styled captain in the Fallon Flying Column, led us on day-long tramps up the local mountain, or on expeditions, some of which could take a week, by boat up what we pretended were unexplored rivers.

It was Garry too who created the Fallon orchestra, which he would solemly conduct, wearing an old pair of tails and using a riding crop as his baton, with Beethoven on the old record player and the rest of us pretending to play, at the appropriate moments, on the fake instruments he had made (very skilfully) from cardboard and string (my clarinet was a Moselle winebottle).

The second eldest, Brian, was the intellectual in what was a fairly bright family, and would read to us for hours at night. He could recite (Il Penseroso) by heart, although we preferred (The Count of Monte Cristo) and (The Three Musketeers). From him we learnt Edward Lear, and chunks of (The Ancient Mariner) which I can recite to this day.

When the two eldest left for university in Dublin, the third brother, Conor took over. He organised fierce games of touch rugby in the winter and Test Match cricket in the summer, in which we had to be the full, current line-up – the 1955 series between England and South Africa was a particularly arduous one for us, playing all day between the cowpats in a glorious summer.

Each of them in his different way was very disciplined, forcing the younger ones to learn properly. We always had guns around the house, but my brothers, rather than my father, set the rules which we younger ones learnt – and we respected them. Niall, the fourth brother, taught us to fish, making Padraic and I practise our casting until our arms ached. Salmon rivers were beyond our reach, but we caught brown trout by the creel-load and, in the season, fishing off the rocks, some fine sea-bass.

Later, while at university, we all continued to be best friends, spending week-ends fishing, or summer holidays sailing. Marriage and children for all six of us inevitably created other interests and pressures, but never loosened the tight, unspoken, relationship between all of us.

In later life, particularly after the death of both our parents, we made conscious efforts to get together for the big occasions: a brother's 40th, 50th or, nowadays, 60th birthday, when we would all meet up for a long week-end, usually in France. The relationship has never altered, the bonds from those early days as strong as ever.

Anne de Courcy, journalist and author of *1939: The Last
Season, Circle: The Life of Edith, Machioness of Londonderry*,
currently writing a biography of Diana Mosley.

●

Proposals, fall into a number of different categories.
There is the Proposal Romantic, the Proposal
Cautious, even the Non-Proposal (seen in its most classic
form in the Jagger-Jerry alliance).

The most dangerous of all, undoubtedly, is the Proposal Reneged-on – and I'm not just thinking of Cecil
Parkinson. You may remember the case of the district
nurse jilted by a nearby village doctor took details of their
four-year affair, including a sheaf of fancy pictures he
had taken of her during a Kenya safari, to the General
Medical Council.

'He had cold feet, and he wasn't going to marry me,' she
said in this modern substitute for the breach of promise
case, adding, as she poured out dates, times, and the
distress it had caused her; 'I don't want to be malicious,
just truthful.' What it did for wildlife tours I don't know,
but the doctor was suspended for nine months.

Most people remember where they made or received a
proposal. Tony Benn proposed to his wife on a park-
bench.

Clearly not only a romantic politically, he then went on
to buy the bench for £30, embellishing it with a plaque to
commemorate the event; and installed it in the Benn

181

garden (as a safe seat one is tempted to say).

My own first proposal came when sitting in the back seat of an aeroplane built for two. As far as categories went, it was a bit of a hybrid.

'Say you'll marry me,' he shouted over his shoulder, pointing the little plane into a terrifying dive (we were above the Isle of Wight at the time) 'or else...' As Cowes zoomed up to meet us I realised only one answer was possible.

As keen students of the question 'Romantic' will already have noticed, this one was a mixture of the Rhett Butler ('Say Yes, Damn You!' school) and the Pre-emptive Strike, the whole lightly coated with the flattering implication that life without the loved one is not worth living.

It also contained – though I was too scared at the time to notice – one classic ingredient of the Proposal Passionate: a sensation of total helplessness in the face of another's overwhelming determination, examples of which abound throughout romantic fiction.

There is Jane Eyre, listening transfixed to Mr Rochester. 'You – you strange, almost unearthly thing! – I love you as my own flesh. You, Jane, I must have you for my own – entirely my own. Will you be mine? Say yes, quickly.'

Or Catherine Gaskin, queen of the lending library shelves, whose hero Lieutenant Andrew Maclay declaims (in Sara Dane) 'You've driven me crazy – witch! I don't sleep nights thinking about you. And I keep my watches like a drunken fool. I can tell you it's been hell! Sara, will you promise to marry me and let me have my peace back again?'

In strict contrast is the Proposal Matter-of-Fact, where

peace has clearly not gone missing for a single second. Listen to this choice example from Daphne du Maurier's Rebecca, whose anonymous heroine hears her wildest dreams come true in words only fractionally more arousing than a British Rail platform announcement.

'So that's settled, isn't it?' he said, going on with his toast and marmalade, 'Instead of being companion to Mrs Van Hopper you become mine, and your duties will be almost exactly the same. I also like new library books, and flowers in the drawing room, and bezique after dinner. And someone to pour out my tea. The only difference is that I don't take Taxol, I prefer Eno's, and you must never let me run out of my particular brand of toothpaste.'

In love, it is often better to travel hopefully than to arrive. Hence the Proposal Cynical, somewhat akin in sentiment to the famous Groucho Marx definition of exclusivity. ('I wouldn't want to join the sort of club that would have me as a member') and here expressed by Ralph Walsh Emerson.

'The accepted and betrothed love has lost the wildest charm of his maiden in her acceptance of him. She was Heaven whilst he pursued her as a star; she cannot be Heaven if she stoops to such a one as he.'

A sub-category here is the Near Miss, perhaps the most familiar of all male excuses. 'Marry you said Candide' 'Those words have opened my eyes to the imprudence of my conduct. Alas, dear idol of my life, I am not deserving of your goodness. Cunegonde is yet living...'

'My wife.'

Few of us will be at the receiving end of the proposal Regal. Here is the 18-year-old Queen Victoria describing Albert's acceptance.

'We embraced each other over and over again, and he was so kind, so affectionate. Oh! to feel I was, and am, loved by such an Angel as Albert was too great delight to describe! He is perfection; perfection in every way...'

Even the Proposal Regal opens with modest flutterings and veiled hints ('I said to Albert I thought he must be aware why I wished them to come here'); but today ritual hesitations are no longer a part of the mating game.

Here is Jilly Cooper's version of the Bed and Breakfast Proposal – her heroine, Emily, meets the impossible Rory at a party on Friday evening, goes to bed with him the same night and on Sunday, after a particularly golden moment in their 48-hour relationship, he prosposes to her.

'I'm bored with living in sin,' he said a couple of hours later. 'Let's get married.'

'I looked at him incredlously, reeling from the shock.

'Did you say you wanted to marry me?' I whispered. 'You can't – I mean, what about all those other girls after you? You could marry anyone. Why me?'

'I'm kinky that way,' he said. 'I'll try anything once.'

As a justification of the two-night stand this glimpse of a busy weekend in Fulham could not be bettered. But back in the days when the Big O was merely one more capital letter, the blinding power of passion was just as apparent. One of the most erotically-charged sentences in all literature is, for me, the moment after Elizabeth Bennet has finally accepted Darcy. 'They walked on without knowing in what direction.'

For the true Proposal Romantic contains not only limitless love, with its scent of gardenia petals, its dazzling fountains of desire, but hope, joy, promise; and the sense of a wider world. May you never have to ask in vain.

Ben Kingsley, actor who shot to fame playing *Ghandi*, stars in Steven Spielberg's latest film, *Schindler's List* and is also one of the stars of *Dave* with Kevin Kline.

•

What I did for Love. 'I let go'.

Benny Green, vagabond saxophonist, lyricist and author of twenty seven books, his BBC Radio Two programme has run for seventeen years. He is currently working on three books.

●

In the early summer of 1952 I took a job in Roy Fox's band, largely for lack of anything better to do. There was nothing much happening for me in London, the promise of £3 a night sounded inviting enough, and I would have for company one of my closest friends, my fellow-saxophonist Harry Klein.

We had, however, been warned by previous members of the orchestra that getting blood out of a stone was a genteel hobby compared to getting money out of Roy. Once upon a time he had been a major showbiz figure, but now he was in steep decline, with an orchestra composed mostly of eccentric second-division players.

The tour consisted of a town a night until we reached Glasgow, where we were due to pitch camp for the obligatory fortnight at Green's Playhouse. I thought it most considerate of Roy when he decided that, as the run up to Scotland was too gruelling to do in a day, we would set off in the coach a day early and stop over in Manchester.

I should make it perfectly clear that at the beginning of the tour I was not even remotely in love with anyone, except of course myself. All fourteen musicians in the band knew girls with whom we were on friendly terms, but these were the kind of liaisons which, it was tacitly agreed between the consenting parties, would never lead to anything permanent, except occasionally to a divorce.

When the itinerary for the tour was handed to us, Klein studied it and reminded me that I had talked of a girl I knew in Manchester. Did she have a friend? It was agreed that when we arrived in the town we would look her up. You never knew. I made it clear to him that there was nothing special about this acquaintanceship. It was just a girl I knew. Klein said he was glad to hear it. He said he didn't want his leisure time ruined with any lovesick small talk. I dropped the girl a line, told her of our impending visit, and left it at that.

We arrived in Manchester in the early evening (this was in the days before the motorways). The members of the band dispersed, and Klein and I took a cab to the girl's address. Everything was in low key. Neither of us took much pleasure in long road journeys, and considered that there was no provincial town remotely to be compared with London. The one consolation was that we had a job, that was all.

While all these thoughts were going through my head, the cab stopped outside a slightly bedraggled green-grocer's corner shop. We found the side door of the house and rang the bell. With this tiny action ended the first part of the escapade, the sane, normal part. We heard galloping noises inside the house, as though some-one were running for dear life. The galloping grew louder, until at last the door was flung open. Through it whizzed a white lace cannonball which crashed into me, wrapped itself around me, and generally behaved as though it were Mafeking and I the relieving force.

Even as I coped with the cascade of kisses, I saw Klein's

astonished face out of the corner of my eye. I inclined my head as well as I could, as if to say to him, 'Look, I'm as flabbergasted by all this as you are', but I don't think to this day he believes me.

I now fell wildly, utterly in love. By the time I had extricated myself from the cannonball, I had already reached the conclusion that the path of my life had now been fully charted.

The next twelve hours were blissful but unreal, and I will pass over them because there are some human moods and experiences which are beyond words. Troths were plighted, promises made, and I remember an attempt to consummate the affair in the stockroom of the shop, on a bed of beetroot sacks, flanked by hillocks of cabbages. By the time I walked drunkenly along the road looking for a taxi or a late night bus, it was past five in the morning. In a few hours we were due to move on to points north and an assignation with a dance hall in Sunderland. When Klein asked me how I had got on, I told him that if he wished, he could be my best man, at which he burst into hysterical laughter and informed the rest of the band that I was ill.

It turned out to be one of those curiously ill-fated tours. At Harwich, Roy Fox put his foot into a cow-pat and sprained his ankle. In Leith, our Canadian second trombonist became so terrified by the air of violence in the town, imagined or not, that he went out shopping and returned with a swordstick. This gesture of unilateral rearmament brought about a visit from the local constabulary, who were only partly convinced when Roy told them that in deference to local customs, the band was rehearsing a sword-dance routine. And at the Beach Ballroom in Aberdeen, the local grass widow, an eccentric lady called Olive, suggested I decamp from the band that night and come and live with her, and in return for any light duties I might perform I would receive a salary of ten pounds a week. At first I thought she was a farceur, but when she handed me her gold wrist watch as a surety of her good intentions. I realised that I had a genuine offer on my hands.

During the band's break, she and I sat on wooden chairs arguing the issue, and I became so involved in the struggle between lust and duty that I never noticed that the band was back on the stand. Thirteen of them were sitting in their places, headed by Roy, and they were all following the debate with fascination. I re-joined the ranks with the issue still unsettled but when, at the end of the dance, Olive came to collect me I submitted willingly enough.

Three hours later I was once again wandering drunkenly along a strange street looking for a taxi to take me back to our hotel. Olive, who was not an ungenerous girl, had given me a pound for my fare, but I ended up thumbing a lift from a lorry. Klein was waiting up to see how I had fared. When I told him about the offer, and how I had decided not to accept it, he told me I was mad, turned over and instantly began to snore, leaving me lying there in a whirl of romantic confusion.

Olive's last words to me were that she would come to Glasgow and stay with me once we arrived. This was a prospect which filled me with a certain sense of foreboding, because Olive was a demanding lady and five years in the profession had left me rather out of condition. So when we reached Kirkcaldy in the afternoon, to find an empty unattended ballroom, I took the opportunity to get some exercise.

The band's singer, a chap called Tony somebody, who later went on to national fame, if that is the right word, with the Black and White Minstrel Show, had once been on Sheffield Wednesday's books, and he and I had no difficulty in taking on the rest of the band. Unfortunately, while executing a complicated shimmy with the ball, I sprained my ribs, and spent the next week with a repugnant green oilskin sheet stuck across my chest. What would Olive say when she saw it?

But Olive never turned up, and I never heard from her again. Some years later, retracing my steps with another band, I made some inquiries and learned that she had gone to rejoin her husband in America.

Her failure to lighten the gloom of Glasgow set off a chain of reactions within me, the first of which was to rip off the detested green oilskin. The second was to treat myself to a new paperback edition of the Journals of Arnold Bennett. The third was to remind myself that I was passionately in love with someone two hundred miles away.

By this stage of our tour, industrial relations inside the band were sinking fast. Roy's policy of paying us once a week for only five or six nights work meant that we were all now so deep in that none of us could see how we would ever escape.

The crunch came at the end of the first week at the Playhouse. Roy, who now owed me the huge sum of £33, surreptitiously slipped me six fivers during the Latin-American medley. The thought instantly occurred to me that this was as good as it was every going to get, and that if I allowed matters to drift on, the debt would quickly grow to unmanageable proportions. There was only one course of action left to me. I would have to leave the band, here and now.

During the band break I told Roy that my grandmother had died and that I would have to return to London instantly. Strictly speaking this was quite true: my grandmother had turned over in bed one night in the summer of 1936 and handed in her dinner pail. But Roy would not hear of my leaving.

'How am I expected to find a replacement in mid-tour?' he asked.

So there the matter lay, with Roy refusing to let me go and I refusing to stay.

That night I conferred with Klein. We analysed the situation as follows: There were two offers on the table. There was the business of true love in Manchester, and there was the offer of a tenner a week from Aberdeen. Which one to go for? Klein advised Aberdeen because, as he rightly pointed out, once I left Roy I would have no visible means of support. But my instinct told me otherwise. My instinct in those days was always infallible. Infallibly wrong, and I decided to steal away to Manchester.

Klein could not understand this. 'You walk out of a three quid a night job AND you turn your back on a tenner a week – and all found – to go for a strictly amateur engagement. Why?'.

I could not explain why. I only knew that the impulse to be rid of the band was now uncontrollable, and that if I took up Olive's offer, I might end up in a kilt.

So Klein agreed to aid and abet me in my flight, which had, of course, to be concealed from Roy. Klein, who had toured around much more than I, knew a local saxophonist only too willing to take my place. The deal was done, and one afternoon, while Roy was asleep in his room down the corridor, I sneaked off to the railway station, carrying one saxophone, one typewriter and a carrier bag crammed with dirty washing. I wired the girl my time of arrival and, when the train pulled in, there she was waiting. Mother Courage in high heels. I felt greatly elated by my act of recklessness, and it was several days before I began to admit that the course of true love never runs smooth. I took a train home with the dirty washing untouched.

The rest of that year was not an easy one, and it was not until just before Christmas that I joined Ronnie Scott and found myself in regular employment again. Some years later I fell in love again, properly this time, married and lived happily ever after.

I still see Klein from time to time. He says he knows of cases where a man has spurned an income for the sake of romance, but that I remain the only fool he has ever heard of who turned down TWO incomes for it.

If anyone reading this true account of youthful indiscretion happens to know where Olive is, perhaps they could get in touch. I figure she still owes me £1.43 for one seventh of a week's work, less the pound for the taxi.

Frank Delaney, acclaimed author and broadcaster, his books include *My Dark Rosaleen, Sins of the Mothers*. His new book is called *Telling the Pictures*.

•

Realistically, the things we do for love mostly have nothing to do with amorous romance. We contribute our loving in a tight enough circle of children, parents, long-term partners and their relatives. To these, our history of undemonstrativeness and restraint allows us to make expressions of love along a scale from tender to respectful. In most other ways we restrict: expressions of love, however non-romantic, are not permitted to colleagues, neighbours and, most regrettably, siblings. The thing I did for love attacked this spore in our emotional culture, but I did not know I was doing it, and only now can I see it with any clarity: as with the old box Brownie cameras of childhood, the negative has taken a long time to develop.

I grew up as a child of the two deadly 'C's, Calvinism and Catholicism, that so inhibited our feelings in the northwest of Europe. The youngest boy of a large family, I eventually, wordlessly, watched the youngest girl die of cancer in her early forties: she was ten years older than me.

Although it was not my first bereavement by death — my father had died several years earlier — it was, and remains, my most important and powerful. It comes back to me frequently, not through the natural sadness of it, or the terrible poignancy – she had five children and the dearest of natures – but through what it taught me about the 'L'-word.

At the funeral, something odd had surfaced inside me, a curious sense of self-importance in all the confusion. Obviously I stifled it, afraid of that baser kind of egoism with which overbearing people appropriate family events. And there seemed no reason why any unusual intensity should apply. We had had no more than a fairly 'ordinary' relationship, similar to those of all families I thought I knew, she lived in Britain, I in Dublin, and we met only once every two years or so. However, warmth had always run between us.

The emotion I felt at the graveside so puzzled and threw me that I began to return to it long afterwards, and gradually I figured out that far from being a rabid kind of self-centredness, this was a formative component. A 'life event' had happened to me, and I could learn from it, grow under its instruction.

This slow realisation may have been some kind of delayed shock, some strange, postponed mourning. When I finally let it out of its box, every texture of the funeral then rushed back at me, and with it a new and searing set of affections for my dead sister's face everywhere or, from a taxi window, a girl who walked like her; heard on the radio a rarely-played Gracie Fields song that she had whacked out on the piano with a fair imitation of Gracie's leathery sinuses; met a man with three sons who each had names my sister had given her boys, my nephews; found in a book a birthday card she sent me when I was twenty; and in the bottom of a suitcase a handkerchief she had given me many years earlier. All this happened within one week but it was now eight years since she died.

When I interrogated this sudden, delayed remembering, I wondered whether it had come on with a rush simply because something within me decided it was time to let go. Or – was this unfinished business, although I had wept enough at the time, or so I thought?

One day's events in particular overwhelmed me. The morning contained nothing to warn me; no party, nor woman-row the night before, none of that inexplicable gloom when I woke up; and at the other end of the scale, no sign of the more dangerous foe, elation. In a noon of glorious sunshine, I left a village where I was doing some research in north Wales and caught the train for London. By the time I reached the dining-car, I was close to tears, a completely unusual situation to this day: I, too, have the locker-room credentials of all men in my generation from these islands.

Several exercises prove useful in such situations: recall the list of tasks facing me when I got back to London; make a note to check with my secretary as to whether A, D and C need any further attention; was the VAT inspection agreed: thus, the iron of mundanity seeped into the soul.

The mettle snapped after lunch when I settled to the crossword. Two clues, I cannot recall them precisely but they may have been something like 'Gracie Fields's favourite houseplant' and 'egg container'. The answers were 'Aspidistra' and, savagely, 'ovaries'. This word lashed out even though the details of my sister's illness were kept from me by the daft secrecies of this emotionally maladroit family system that large Irish Catholic families have. Ovaries have to do with procreation, and procreation has to do with sex.

In order to compose myself I used another old business trick. I wrote down at random an intensifying progression of queries, in order to try and edit down to one question, and thereby get close to one answer, a kind of homing in on the nucleus of the problem. Like a rare game of Patience it all came out. Why had the passage of time not erased this dreadful, bereft feeling?

The answer distilled reluctantly to four letters on the page – that word again, a word I never heard in my ordinary family growing up in the Irish countryside, not even once. 'Love' in my background was as taboo an expression as any of the usual four-letter ones. In my time, fathers did not 'love' their sons; parents didn't 'love' their children, not where I came from. Siblings didn't 'love' each other. No such thing. Stuff, if not nonsense. Nobody was to blame; that was the way of the world.

The rest became immediately apparent. I had never 'loved' my sister, therefore I never mourned her. Obviously, all the sudden recollections of her had come – that is to say, I only began to mourn her fully – when, eight years after her funeral, some part of me acknowledged that it was all right to use the word 'love'. Anger broke out, followed by a sense of shame at coming from a national society where such familial reticence was the norm. It calmed down soon, but I have never seen any family relationship in the same light since. All such withholdings of love gouge flaws as deep as geological faults in all families who have them.

My sister whom I now love (note: *love* with no parentheses), my dead sister, who had cancer finally in every available organ of her body, informs much that I do. In two long novels and a novelette I have been unable not to represent her in some way, and the novel I am writing at the moment will be suffused with the loving principles I was never told about, and never allowed by the general culture to practise when she was alive.

But I try to practise them now – even if I, like most people, still have difficuty in getting the words along that difficult, often taboo-blocked canal from the heart to the lips. If we love someone, we should tell them.

Why not? Dr Johnson, an Englishman to the tacks in the soles of his boots, and therefore by definition stiff-rigid in the upper lip, was able, in the eighteenth century, to lunge across a London dining-table to a man he had but recently met and say warmly, 'Give me your hand sir, for I have taken a liking to you'. Terrific. Brave! I am with him all the way – even if it means unsound tear-ducts whenever I hear a cracked recording of *The Biggest Aspidistra in the World*.

Paul Nicholas, star of *Just Good Friends* singer and co-producer
of *Grease*, was one of the original stars of *Hair* and *Cats*.
Recently starred in a tour of *Barnum*.

•

I'm tempted to tell you about the time I woke up next to
a transvestite – the big feet gave him away – but on
second thoughts I'll tell you how I seduced my wife.

I was on tour with the original production of *Hair* and
I'd fancied Linzi for weeks, but I was too shy to do
anything about it. I'd been going out with a friend of hers
because I couldn't pluck up courage to ask Linzi out.

Finally, in Manchester, I managed to install myself in
the room above hers in the flats we were allocated. One
night – about two o'clock in the morning actually – I
knocked on her door, asking if I could borrow some glue
because some piece of furniture in my room had broken.
It must have sounded quite ridiculous, but Linzi, who is
an extremely practical person, obviously thought she'd
found a kindred spirit. She invited me in and we've been
stuck together ever since.

Marcelle d'Argy Smith editor of *Cosmopolitan* contributes regularly to TV and radio and is the author of *Men, Women and Me* from which the poem in this book is taken.

•

Though certain men had tendered bids
 I'd never really thought of kids
My life lacked vital discipline
To fit a tiny baby in.
Then I saw Katie...

I'd put up that familiar fight.
I'll do it when the timing's right
Which is a silly thing to say
As I thought that September day
When I met Katie.

A five-pound wondrous happening
Delivered in the Lindo Wing,
St Mary's. The most perfect child.
They gave her to me and Kate smiled
When I held Katie.

There was an instant sweet rapport formed in the Lindo
 corridor between that new-born babe and me.
I loved her instantaneously
When I held Katie.

I talk though she were my own
But darling Kate belongs to Joan
   my special New York/London friend
   with whom I stayed for months on end
Next door to Katie.

She's like a miniature Holbein
She hugs me and she feels like mine.
Oh sometimes feelings half-suppressed
   well silently within my breast
When I hug Katie…

I've so loved watching Katie grow
She's four years old this year you know
My life still lacks the discipline
To fit a tiny baby in
So I share Katie…

Maggie Goodman, journalist and magazine editor, former
deputy editor of *Cosmopolitan*, created and became launch
editor of *Company Magazine* and was also launch editor of *Hello!*

•

I used to be a normal person. I wore normal clothes,
used normal language, spent normal weekends with
friends and family and went on normal holidays in cars
and hotels. And then I met Mad Boatman. He had a
dinghy and something called a surf boat with a shiny,
slippery surface, and he spent weekends pitching these
against the elements off the grey Harwich coast. Newly
divorced, his excuse was that this was something to keep
his teenage boys amused – better than going to the zoo.
The boys, however, soon lost interest and I became the
object of his fanatical desires.

The first time I went in the surf boat, a gust of wind
blew me silently off it. But Mad Boatman, manicly playing with his sails, didn't even notice until a passing helms-
man drew his attention to this pathetic creature waving
not drowning.

It was a cold and wet romance built on panic and relief,
violent argument and hysterical laughter, sweet nothings
inaudible against the wind, physical attractions lost
beneath waterproof layers of Michelin Man proportions.

Then everything changed. Mad Boatman decided to
build a boat. A big boat. An ocean-going trimaran with
cabins and galleys and enough room to take six people

round the world. Mad Boatman did have a day-job but he assured me this little project could be knocked off in a couple of years of weekends. Small sacrifice I thought.

It took seven years. Seven years of weekends and holidays in a Thames-side shed peopled by fellow maniacs who could have walked straight out of a David Storey play. Mostly I left him to it because on my rare visits to the shed I was overcome with gloom at the amount still to be done. The coast of England is littered with the hulls of half-finished boats and I was guilty of little faith.

But I stayed around, occasionally enticing Mad Boatman away for a holiday (flotilla sailing in Turkey, what else?), until the great day of the launch in St Katherine's Dock. Rashly I promised unlimited champagne for the party and everyone we'd ever met seemed to have found out.

Thus began stage three of this sea-going love affair. The Mad Boatman could take more holidays than me, so he was forever setting off with fellow mariners and arranging to meet me in far-off harbours. Problem here was his enduring optimism even in the face of the first two laws of the sea: everything takes longer than you imagine, and something always goes wrong.

'Take the ferry to Roscoff and I'll meet you,' he'd say, meaning every word. Or 'I'll definitely be in Gibraltar waiting for you on Friday.'

Fog, calms, storms, fouled propellers – even bad hangovers – inevitably intervened. Bitter experience forced me to set up complicated communication arrangements with bemused third parties and also insist on not leaving home until he's actually arrived at an agreed destination and promised to stay there.

Then there's the cash-flow problem. Whoever invented the phrase about sailing being like standing under a cold shower tearing up five pound notes was seriously misinformed. You can't even get a grommet for five pounds. In its short life, this boat has had three engines (yes it *is* a sailing boat), new mast, new railings, new sails and every single navigation instrument updated to the state of the art. I couldn't bear to work out the cost but it has to be more than hiring a luxury yacht to sail round the world.

I am not alone in my love-hate relationship with Mad Boatman and his floating toy. Friends clamour to join me in being cold, wet, frightened, uncomfortable and shouted at. And they come back for more. As I do.

Sometimes I dream of a mellower future where the boat is moored permanently in a picturesque French harbour and makes only the occasional foray into the deeps. But only yesterday this fantasy was shattered. 'I'm thinking,' said Mad Boatman, 'of doing the Trans-Atlantic next year'.

**Andy Ripley, former Rugby star, capped 24 times for England, author of *Ripley's Rugby Rubbish*, cycled for ROC and works for a bank.**

•

It was the twelfth of July 1993. A big day. Exactly 499 years ago, Lucia Pacioli had written the definitive accountancy text book *Summa d'Arithmetica*. Wild. Exactly 303 years ago, King Billy crossed the Boyne, and 204 years ago less 2 days, the guys in the funny hats had stormed the Bastille. It's also the mid-point between my daughters' birthday parties. Fascinating. See what I mean. It's a big one babes, the old twelfth of July and no mistake.

So there I was on the good old twelfth, hanging out in Terrace Dining Room A of the House of Commons at the Research into Ovarian Cancer launch of the Trans Britain Bike Ride. Cos that's the kind of guy I am. As an ageing micro celeb you get the chance to visit Terrace Dining Room A. Jealous? Phew? I betchoo are.

Anyway I was riveting George Ayling (married to Pat Ayling) about how a cubic foot of water is equal to 6.24 gallons and he was fascinating me about the price of fuel. When up saunters this babe and says, 'Hi, I'm Frankie and I want you to write about love and ovarian cancer.' Easy peasy stuff, I said, but do you Frankie know how many litres there are in the Imperial gallon? She kids, didn't have a clue.

209

Men don't get ovarian cancer. 5000 women in the UK every year do, 4000 die. There are no obvious symptoms until it's spread. If you catch it before it's spread there's a 90% success rate with existing treatment. The current blood test isn't perfect – it needs fine tuning, it needs £200,000 a year for five years. Sadly and happily it seems it needs blokes on bikes to raise money.

John Cullen's mother, Pamela, died of ovarian cancer. To channel his grief and to prevent other men feeling how he felt about their loved women being snatched by this silent killer. He set up a fund-raising bike ride from John O'Groats to Land's End. I joined him.

My eldest sister had a hysterectomy in her early forties, quite by chance the surgeon found she had uterine cancer, a close and nasty cousin of cancer of the ovaries. She got lucky and so did I because I love her and I want her here.

Oh yes, Frankie, there are 4.2 litres in a gallon even on the twelfth of July.

Jan Etherington journalist and writer, she is scriptwriter for television's successful sitcom *Second Thoughts* which she co-writes with her husband, Gavin Petrie.

•

When I recall the evening I was certain we'd be alone, I still wince. I was vamping precariously along the hall, wearing something diaphanous and balancing two chilled glasses of Sancerre when the front door opened and five 16-year-old boys exploded in. Only the fact that I was passing the broom cupboard at the time saved me from relinquishing for ever my role as a sensible parent and figure of considerable authority.

Trying to hang on to your sex life when there are teenagers in the house requires the tenacity of a tax inspector and the ingenuity of a *Times* crossword compiler.

When they were small there were other problems, but at least they went to bed when it was dark. And even if they did get up again you had a bit of warning – like a yell or a clunk as they fell out of the cot. Also, tiny kids don't know about rude bits, so if they spotted you swinging from the chandelier while wearing a warm smile and a bit of tulle, they'd probably assume you were re-enacting a scene from *The Jungle Book*.

Teenagers know all about these things, making it more difficult to remain a woman of mystery. 'What's that?' enquired my daughter, as I was sneaking something through the hall in a plain brown carrier bag. 'Just something I needed,' I said as I struggled with her, but she's stronger than I am. 'Ooh! Proper stockings,' she hooted, 'and a suspender belt!'

'It's a surprise for his birthday,' I said without thinking.

'Wouldn't he rather have a book of *Punch* cartoons?' she asked, but she knew what I meant.

And all this baloney about 'bring a bit of spice back into your relationship – eating in bed is almost impossible without running the assault course of your inquisitive offspring. 'Is this asparagus?' 'Yes.' 'Can we have some?' 'No.' 'Where are you going with it?' 'We are going to eat in bed.' 'You're not ill, are you?' 'No.' 'I'm only allowed to eat in bed when I'm ill.'

Time alone together takes on even more urgency when you form a new relationship while your children are teenagers. I married for the second time when my son was 13 and my daughter 15. I heard my daughter on the phone once, 'Yes, they're always snogging in the kitchen. God – it's embarassing!' My son once exploded when he caught us in a clinch. 'Why can't you be a normal mother and not be in love?'

I can't remember when we had an uninterrupted early night. 'We're having an early night,' I announce.

'Are you tired?' asks my son.

'You don't have to be tired to have an early night.' My daughter tells him knowingly.

Even when you think they're all out, they're never gone completely. 'Mum! Where are you?' Gasp for breath. 'In bed.' 'Why, what's up? 'Can I come in?' Come in first. Knock later. 'Oh, sorry!' 'Can't you damn well knock before you barge in!' 'Sorry, I just wanted some money for the club tonight.' 'We're trying to watch *Wildlife on*

*One!*' I storm, attempting to disentangle myself from the duvet. Thank God we've got a television in the bedroom, otherwise I would have no excuse for my wantonness.

But why should I need an excuse? I'm not ready to give up the pleasures of the flesh yet. So why do I have to apologise for a perfectly natural urge in what is still a relatively young woman.

Well one of the reasons is when I was a kid, I couldn't imagine anyone over the ancient age of 20 actually placing themselves in a recumbent position with a person of the opposite gender and indulging in those practices we'd been told about in our hygiene class.

My parents were openly affectionate but kissing and holding hands were different from 'going the whole way'. 'Don't let boys rub against you,' said bossy Eunice firmly when we joined the local lads for ballroom dancing classes. 'There could be consequences,' I rushed home and looked up consequences. How could I protect myself from 'logical conclusion' I wondered?

So although I insist I don't have any hang-ups about sex, I remember thinking how ludicrous it was to believe that grown ups, who were obviously past any kind of emotion except unreasonable anger, should be indulging in an activity designed for the young. And as my children have always thought of me as a figure of fun, I'm sure they can't imagine anything dafter or more hysterical than their mother in the grip of passion.

And, yes, dammit I'm embarrassed when they catch me at it, or as near as makes no difference. And even when they're miles away, they're still indulging in the sport of *parentus interruptus*. Phone rings. 'Mum, please can you pick me up from Woking? I've missed the last train... Mum are you okay?' 'I'm a bit out of breath. I had to run for the phone.' She knows damn well I wouldn't be running from anywhere but the bottom of the blankets at 1 am.

But only last week I realised that maybe I'd got the message across. We were watching the late film when I heard the Doc Marten boots of my daughter and her cronies clumping down the hall. 'Better knock,' I heard her whisper at the living room door. 'They're probably at it on the sofa.' We sprang apart just in time. 'You two are up late. Isn't it time you were in bed?' said my daughter disapprovingly.

I'm constantly living with the realisation that I've let my children down by embarrassing them and their friends with unseemly displays of affection, and loving every minute of it.

Julia Langdon, journalist, author and political commentator
contributes to national newspapers, radio and television and is
political consultant to *GMTV*.

•

I f all politicians are mad – and no sane person can really
have much doubt about that – then anyone who
chooses to spend half of the day and most of the night
working in the company of loonies must be pretty far
gone along the trail. Why do it? Why, for love of course.

For love, for toothpaste and for tomato ketchup. The
latter two relate to another sort of love and we'll get to
them in a minute. The main point is that one can only
stand such a crazy job if one truly has a passion for
politics. Otherwise, it would drive you mad.

I rather like it when people ask what I do for a living. "I
hang around in bars," I reply somewhat smugly. This has
the virtue of being true, but is additionally attractive
because it is ever so slightly shocking. It's like when the
mother-in-law's friends used to ask what I did before I
was married. "Like sleep around, you mean?" I would
challenge them, for the hell of it. Ah, but that was long
ago when girls like I was weren't expected to "do anything", let alone hang around in bars.

But that, dear reader, is the lot of the parliamentary
lobby correspondent. You want to know how the Government's plans are going down? You go to the bars. You
wish to hear the gossip? Then perhaps a few hours in the

215

early evening around the main watering holes. You would like to find out what ministers think is going on? Take them out to lunch or dinner and talk about it over a glass of wine. And as for what is really happening? Well, there's nothing to beat a few drinks after the 10 pm vote when the atmosphere is usually really pretty relaxed.

The wine virgins amongst us are quite careful about all this booze, not least in order to remain wise. That means you have to remember what people tell you, otherwise the exercise would have been fairly pointless in the first place. A love of politics involves a relish in relating its intricacies.

And it is important, too, to remain sober and keep your wits about you, not only because some insonsiderate proprietor might ask you to put some of this down in print. There is also the possibility of the midnight emergency.

These come in many forms. Sometimes it is just an unexpected political wriggle that has emerged in the morning blats. Sometimes it is the whisper of the rumour that may bring down a minister, or even a government. Sometimes they telephone you, these barmy politicians, in the early hours of the morning to pour out their hearts about either their policies or their popsies and you hear them out, you let them talk it through.

Out of love, really. Love of politics because it's never dull and it matters. Love of politicians because, be they great or small, they are only human. Love of the very humanity of it all.

… And because you have to buy toothpaste and tomato ketchup. "Don't use too much of that!" I shout at those I love. "Don't you realise I have to go to work to earn the money to buy those things?"

"But you love it," they say and they're right.

Alan Bleasdale, acclaimed playwright whose many successes
include *Boys From the Blackstuff* and the award winning
*GBH*, he is currently producing a new series of plays
for Channel 4 from new writers.

•

Thirty nine years ago, in 1954, when I was eight years
old, I lost my faith in God and replaced Him immediately with Monica Haygarth.

It was an easy choice. For a start, God was *never* there
when I needed him, and Monica Haygarth sat next but
one to me in class. Visiting priests told us regularly that
God was everywhere, but I had never seen him. I
couldn't reach out and touch God, whereas I could quite
easily reach out across the fat girl who sat between us and
touch Monica. Although I think she might have hit me if
I had.

Furthermore, God had done absolutely nothing for
me. Ever. I had prayed and prayed that my Nanna would
get better and she promptly died; I had asked God on
numerous occasions to help me beat Peter Whitehead in
the sports day sprint and every year for three years I had
come second; it was also becoming obvious to me that
prayer was little use in getting Liverpool Football Club
out of the Second Division and, conclusively, however
hard I prayed and however hard I tried, I still hadn't
learnt how to ride a two-wheeler bike. God may have had
a hand in my learning to swim, but I suspect the hands

that really counted belonged to some older lads who pushed me into the deep end at Knotty Ash baths one Saturday morning.

Actually, upon reflection, I think God had a lucky escape. Even He, renowned in some quarters for his Almighty patience, would surely have aimed a sizeable thunderbolt in my direction if I'd pursued and adored Him in the love-sick manner that I was to pursue and adore Monica Haygarth from 1955 to 1963. Over all those years Monica wasn't, to be perfectly frank, a very good God to me but, God knows, I can hardly blame her.

I don't know why I picked her out for worship. I now remember her to be bright, shy, dark haired, pretty but slightly sharp featured in repose. It might have been that, to my delight, Monica wouldn't let Billy Passmore walk with her on the way to and from school, and I hated Billy Passmore. Not only could he ride a bike, he also had blonde Brylcreemed hair and a huge collection of imported American comics that he would only ever let you borrow if money was involved.

Whatever the reason for my choice of veneration, I cannot think of one God-like action that Monica performed that converted me; no miracle with the warm school milk, fancy tricks with the fish fingers and loaves; her wooden desk never did weep salt tears; she did not lay her hands upon my maths book and suddenly I knew my twelve times tables.

Monica Haygarth simply became my God, and there were times when I invested my life in her and her greater glory. She became the constant subject of my bewildering daydreams – or daydream, because there was only one; separate showings but the same film.

I am in a trench like I imagined my father to have been

218

in during the Second World War. However, this is a religious war, and there is heavy fighting among the battalions of under elevens. Every child in my school, St Aloysius Roman Catholic School, has advanced from our assembly hall, through the playground, over the road and into the park. We are behind the railings in Jubilee Park, facing the Protestant troops trapped in Park View School. They refuse to surrender but there is no escape. The school meals van cannot get through and they are slowly starving to death. And damnation. I am a Captain, the leader of the infant and junior troops, the brightest boy in the school. I wear a Captain's moustache and uniform and a brave smile. Monica and all the girls from St Aloysius are behind the front lines in tents on the bowling green, nursing the wounded and cooking in the captured park-keeper's hut. At night, there is no fighting. It is agreed by both sides. At night, my Catholic troops would retire to the wooden dressing rooms once used before the war by footballers in the park at the weekend. And there, in the dip by the bowling green and the shrubs and the sycamore trees, I would sleep in a big double bed. With Monica. For comfort, comfort alone. I was only eight.

And then I was nine, and then I was ten and then I was eleven. And both my God and I passed the eleven plus. Our grammar schools were fifteen miles apart, but, unlike my first fractured relationship with the God who gave me Ash Wednesday and screaming fears of mortality, never answered my prayers or made a live appearance, absence made my heart grow even fonder for Monica.

This hopeless parading puppy love for Monica was, without her ever knowing, of some benefit to me. Rejection and side effects. For a start, she made me extremely fit, because I had to run at a wild gallop two miles a day, Monday to Friday, forty weeks of the year, to get from where my school bus dropped me off to where I knew she would be getting off her bus and turning around the corner to Page Moss shops. Sadly, when I got there, all I could do was catch my breath and pretend to saunter past her with a warm smile, a nonchalant wave and a falsetto "Hy hello". This was because I lived in the opposite direction to her, and also, let's face facts, because for many years she wouldn't let me walk with her. And that included walking slightly behind or in front of her. And I really was too much of a gentle boy to do anything she didn't want me to do. Well, I might do it until she told me not to do it and then I would never do it again.

Monica was also my fundamental reason for finally learning how to ride a bike. Once I could ride a bike, and my parents had saved up to buy me a bike, I could then ride my bike up and down outside her house until it went dark. Or until her father came out of the house and chased me. I must say though that Monica's mother, her grandmother and her younger sister were much more gentle in their approach. They merely laughed at me. Then, one night, Monica came out and told me not to ride up and down outside her house anymore. I tried to sell the bike the next day to a lad called McGillivery, but my mother got upset and words like "HP payments" and "come here while I kill you" came into the conversation.

However, Monica's greatest unknowing triumph was her massive contribution to my tennis skills. This most reluctant of Goddesses made me by far the best bet for Wimbledon in our parish. For one simple reason. The tennis courts in Jubilee Park overlooked Monica Haygarth's house...

The only pain she ever inflicted upon me, other than the continual pain of polite rejection, was the sacred suffering I had to go through every Sunday morning. For Monica was a very devout and serious churchgoer and she always went to eight o'clock Mass. So to see her on the seventh day, and I had to see her, I worshipped for several years at the altar of my false God, taking Communion and feeling unfaithful to the God two pews in front of me and slightly to the side so I could see something of her in profile.

And on and on and on my pathetic suffering and sad vigil and utter devotion continued. I kept diaries during some of those years. I don't know which I'm more ashamed of now – the near illiteracy or the spaniel I see upon the pages.

January 10th, 1960. Full Moon. Got 40 lines in Maths. Got into trouble at dinner. Had a fight with Peter O'Gorman. It was his fault. Dinner was pork and jam roly poly. Liverpool's game against United all ticket. Prices gone up. Ground two and sixpence. Saw Monica, but she was very stuck up today. I don't understand. She was very nice yesterday. Bacon, sausage and egg for tea. And peaches.

March 1st, 1960. Princess Margaret to get married. Cottage pie and semolina. (Ugh!). Didn't see Monica, saw her sister, her sister says she's got chicken pox. Sent her a get well card. Didn't mention not getting a Valentine card. It rained. Had lamb chops and chips for tea.

Friday, 17th March, 1961. Bonney (the headmaster) won't let me drop physics and chemistry, the flaming bum! If it's the last thing I do, I'll get him for it. Mince for dinner with spotted dick. Scored two goals in games. Waited for Monica. She never got off bus. Waited for next three buses. Then went home. St Patrick's Day. When Irish eyes are smiling. I only want one pair of eyes to smile at me. Sausages and mash for tea.

When writing fiction I'm usually careful not to set any dreadful events in April, because I know the temptation to trot out "April is the cruellest month" would be too easy. However, the April of 1961 lived up to all of T.S. Eliot's expectations. For written large in red ink in my diary on Friday the 7th of April is the following: OH BOY! OH BOY! MY RED LETTER DAY! MONICA HAYGARTH SAID SHE WOULD GO OUT WITH ME. ONE OF THE HAPPIEST DAYS OF MY LIFE! AFTER SEVEN YEARS. (I HOPE!!!). THE HAPPIEST DAYS OF MY LIFE: (1) WINNING SCHOLARSHIP. (2) THE DAY WE BEAT THE COLLEGIATE 3-0 AFTER LOSING THE FIRST MATCH 15-1. (3) BEATING LIVERPOOL BOYS 3-2 AND I SCORED A GOAL AND HIT THE BAR. (4) TODAY. PLEASE. PLEASE. PLEASE.

Sunday, 9th April, 1961. Went to 8 o'clock Mass WITH Monica! Said she would definitely go out with me soon. Said she would let me know. Was very nice. I told her a joke and then had to explain it. Played tennis for four hours until nobody else would play. Didn't see Monica.

Wednesday, 19th April, 1961. One of these days I'll understand Monica Haygarth. Nearly two weeks ago she said she would go out with me, and then she avoids me! Top Of The Hit Parade is "You're Driving Me Crazy". And you are, Monica, you are!

Sunday, 23 April, 1961. Went to eight o'clock Mass. Monica wasn't there. Her friend Christine was there. Ended up talking to her for over two hours. Monica told her to tell me that she had made a mistake and didn't want to go out with me and she was very sorry. Christine was very good about it, said she understands how I must feel. But she can't. Went home and stayed in my bedroom all day. Played Elvis's "Now And Then There's A Fool Such As I" over and over again. Didn't have my tea. Told mum I was sick.

…Almost every 31st of December for nine years: Monica's birthday. Hope she got my card. Will next year be my lucky year?!?!

1963 was my "lucky" year. I had, thankfully, stopped writing a daily diary by then, but one of the few entries, for Thursday the 2nd of May, reads "Unbelievably, Monica Haygarth said "yes" – and said she means it this time. Going to see The Beatles, Gerry and the Pace-makers and Roy Orbison on the 26th of May".

I couldn't – or wouldn't confess it at the time, not even to my diary, but I have long since faced up to the reality that firstly, tickets to see the Beatles in Liverpool in the Spring of 1963 were as rare as jobs would become twenty years later and, secondly, Monica was a Beatles fan. Get the picture? Uh-huh. But I didn't. I only had the sound turned up.

We went to see the Beatles. We went to see Laurence of Arabia and West Side Story. One evening I accidentally touched her right breast with my left elbow. Another night we had an argument about God. It was strange arguing about God with someone who had been mine for all those years, for how could I say that I didn't believe in God when I had believed in her for over half my life?

What was much more natural was the terrible shock upon realising that my She-God was a real person with all real people's strengths and weaknesses, delights and frailties. She must have always known that I was a seriously diffident boy with a weakness for genuflection. But I was stunned to find, when I finally looked, that she didn't quite have the raving beauty of Sophia Loren, the sex appeal of Marilyn Monroe, the singing voice of Dusty Springfield and the wit of Lucille Ball.

We went out with each other for three weeks and then at the end of one of our increasingly difficult meetings I never said I would see her again, and she never asked. I stopped going to Church and joined a tennis club. I haven't had a God to look up to ever since.

Many years later, in the mid-seventies, Monica and I met briefly when we were both schoolteachers and married with three children. She was delightful. Witty and warm and far from shy. And she didn't go to Church anymore. I was terribly ashamed that I had, over such a long period, pestered her with my ridiculous attentions. I could only think of the misery it must have been to be her and see me coming.

To my relief and surprise she said that she had, from the very onset, been thrilled by my dedication and glorification; that seeing me half in hiding and waiting was often the highlight of her day. To be adored, even by me, made her feel so special that on many occasions she would wait for me. Before ignoring me all the way home.

I wish that was the happy ending.

But it isn't.

The year immediately after 'The Boys From The Black Stuff' was screened was the worst year of my life; like something out of a cheap and ludicrous melodrama.

My mother had died suddenly, my father had to have major surgery, both my wife's stepfather and her uncle, two good and decent men, died inexorably and painfully of cancer, her sister-in-law was killed in a car crash, and then, almost unbelievably, our eldest boy became very seriously ill. I think I went out of my mind in 1983, and if I didn't, I certainly went out to the off-licence. Walking around town, I could see people looking at me and thinking "Oh lucky man", while inside, I was screaming.

And, as I was saying about cheap melodrama, the very morning that we were to bury my wife's stepfather, the phone rang in our hallway. the front door was open. The funeral cars were waiting in the driveway. I picked the phone up. It was Monica. She was in hospital. She had leukemia. She wanted to see me.

I never went. I sent flowers. I talked to her on the phone. But I never went. And then she died.

I could defend my lack of action at the time. My defence lay in the paragraphs above and, after all, I told myself, I had only seen her for a matter of hours in two decades. People I knew better and loved more were dying all around me, and our son was blacking out up to sixty times a day. Every day. I just didn't think then that I could possibly take any more grief.

Now however, with the passing of the proverbial, the almost complete recovery of my father, the partial recovery of our son, and given the calmness of distance, I've been known to come to the unforgiving conclusion that it was the cruellest thing I have ever done to anyone.

Our Monica who art in Heaven...

© Alan Bleasdale

## THE THINGS WE DO FOR LOVE

If you've enjoyed the wonderful stories in this book you won't be able to resist telling your friends and loved ones how warm, sad, intriguing and hilarious it is. And this will probably mean you have to give them your copy...

Much better to buy another copy(ies) from your local bookshop as the perfect present for someone you love or admire, knowing that the proceeds of each sale go to a very worthy cause... and you get to keep your own book.

Alternatively you can order more copies to be sent to your friend(s) direct from the publisher.

### Blake Publishing Ltd.,
### Cash Sales Department, Bookpoint,
### 39 Milton Park, Abingdon, Oxon, OX14 4TD, UK.

If you have a credit card you may order by telephone: (0235) 831700.

Please enclose a cheque or postal order made payable to Bookpoint Ltd., to the value of the cover price and allow the following for postage and packing:

UK and BFPO – £1.00 for the first book, 50p for the second book and 30p for each additional book ordered up to a maximum charge of £3.00.

OVERSEAS and EIRE – £2.00 for the first book, £1.00 for the second book and 50p for each additional book.

Name _____

Address _____

_____ Postcode _____

Name _____

Address _____

_____ Postcode _____

Name _____

Address _____

_____ Postcode _____